TREATING
CHEMICALLY DEPENDENT
FAMILIES

TREATING CHEMICALLY DEPENDENT FAMILIES
A PRACTICAL SYSTEMS APPROACH FOR PROFESSIONALS

John T. Edwards, Ph.D.

 Hazelden
Publishing

Hazelden
15251 Pleasant Valley Road
Center City, MN 55012
1-800-328-9000
http://www.hazelden.org

Library of Congress Cataloging-in-Publication Data

Edwards, John T.
   Treating chemically dependent families: a practical systems approach for professionals/John T. Edwards.
         p. cm. — (Professional Series)
   Includes bibliographical references (p. 219) and index.
   ISBN 0-935908-56-0
      1. Substance abuse–Treatment. 2. Family psychotherapy.
   I. title. II. Series: Professional series (Minneapolis)
   RC564.E35   1990
   616.86'0651—dc20
                                    90-5111
                                    CIP

ISBN 13: 978-0-935908-56-5

PRINTED IN THE UNITED STATES OF AMERICA

ACKNOWLEDGMENTS

I thank my colleagues who shared their time and expertise in reviewing or editing this manuscript: Jim Palmer, Cecil Yount, Carol Hoffman, and Tab Ballis.

My thanks to Carole Remboldt of the Johnson Institute, who inspired the project and whose professionalism made this a more valuable book for professionals, and to Jim Bitney, whose careful editing added clarity and simplicity to the text.

A special thanks to B.J. McCartin, whose enthusiasm and friendship sparked my own enthusiasm for my work.

And a warm appreciation to Gene Hall, whose understanding of management's role in the healing process continues to delight and challenge me.

To Raynelle Pearson Edwards, whose love
and acceptance saved my life.

CONTENTS

PREFACE

I use the term "alcohol or other drugs" in this book to emphasize that alcohol *is* a drug—just like tranquilizers, cocaine, marijuana, heroin, or any other mind-altering substance. I also often use the term "chemical dependence" because it covers dependence on all these mind-altering drugs and because it's short and simple.

Too often people talk about "alcohol *or* drugs" or "alcohol *and* drugs" as if alcohol were somehow different from drugs and in a category by itself. True, our culture, our government, even our laws, treat alcohol differently from the way they treat other drugs such as pot, crack, or smack. But the symptoms of dependence are essentially the same for all these mind-altering drugs, and there is an urgent need to find ways to prevent or to intervene with their use.

Throughout this book, then, the abbreviation "CD" refers either to chemical dependence (as in "CD problem") or to chemically dependent (as in "CD family member"). Other terms and abbreviations used in this book include:

— *Family*: two or more people bound together by legal, blood, or emotional ties, with enough of a past together to suggest a future together. In a practical and therapeutic sense, a family is whoever the therapist believes is necessary to solve the presenting problems.

— *IP* stands for identified patient, the person in the family who has been initially identified as the chemical user.

—*CD client* or *CD member* refers to the IP.
—*AA* stands for Alcoholics Anonymous.
—*NA* stands for Narcotics Anonymous.
—*Al-Anon* is a self-help organization for family members of alcoholics.
—*Alateen* is a self-help organization for teen-aged family members of alcoholics.
—*Naranon* is a self-help organization for the family of persons who are chemically dependent on drugs other than, but often including, alcohol.
—*Primary treatment* refers to the separate (inpatient or outpatient) treatment of the CD family member. Such treatment generally consists of education, various forms and combinations of group and individual therapy, and usually includes twelve-step groups such as AA or NA.
—*Co-dependence* refers to a recognizable pattern of self-defeating thoughts, attitudes, and behaviors predictably found within many members of chemically dependent families.
—*Primary co-dependent* refers to the family member, usually a spouse or parent, who exhibits the most severe co-dependent symptoms.

For purposes of family treatment, the approach in this book is essentially the same, regardless of the drug(s) of choice of the CD family member. The critical criterion for diagnosis is the effect the drug has on the life of the user and the life of his or her family. The book's working definition of chemical dependence is simple: If a family member's alcohol or other drug use causes problems in the user or in the family, the *family* has a chemical dependence problem. Therefore, in therapy sessions it's best to let the problems do the talking and to avoid hair-splitting definitions that only give rise to resistance and defensive posturing ("I'm not an alcoholic, because an alcoholic is someone who . . . ").

Although this book addresses doing therapy with CD families, therapists can use most of its methods and techniques to treat any dysfunctional family. Experience has shown, however, that many dysfunctions in families—violence and battering, child abuse and/or neglect, adolescent behavioral problems, individual depression, etc.— are, in fact, linked to, or are effects of, chemical dependence. Because chemical dependence is so prevalent, every treatment professional needs at least a basic understanding of how to assess and treat this disorder.

Introduction

This book is about how to do therapy with families in which at least one member is dependent on alcohol or other drugs. It presents approaches and methods for therapists to use in organizing their therapy with chemically dependent (CD) families, makes suggestions for treatment strategies, and offers specific, systems-based techniques ("When the wife cries, hand the tissues to the husband."). This is a clinical guidebook for working with CD families in the early stages of recovery from the disease.

Part One lays the foundations for CD family therapy by giving the principles and goals for the family systems approach. Part Two explains the methods for accomplishing the goals, including common patterns for CD families and suggested strategies for treatment; gives four fundamental techniques for working with CD families; provides a "shopping basket" of additional techniques; and ends with four common traps CD family therapists may fall into and possible ways to avoid them. Part Three offers guidelines for getting families in for therapy and for conducting the first interview. It also discusses common problems to watch for in the middle and ending stages of the therapy.

Being a family clinician for the past twelve years has taught me a personal lesson: What we *know* about chemical dependence and families doesn't help—what does help is what we *do* with what we know. Our knowledge, opinions, and subjective reactions are of no

1

value until they are translated into clinical actions the family can hear, see, and feel. Techniques and methods are the vehicles for this translation; they bring our concepts, theories, and hunches to face-to-face encounters with families, where they can do some good.

This book offers practical ideas and methods by focusing on four key questions:

1. What are CD families like?
2. What is *this* CD family like?
3. What can the therapist do to help the family?
4. How can the therapist do it?

These four questions are addressed within a systems framework. Reduced to its simplest terms, the systems orientation assumes that each member affects the family and that the family affects each member in a reciprocal and dynamic way. It's not hard to grasp this idea, but we can easily miss the systemic process during therapy if we watch the individual dancers and ignore the dance.

The systems orientation by itself is just an interesting abstraction, but when properly applied, it can have payoffs. It helps the therapist make connections between and among different sequences of behavior. For example, the systems orientation helps the therapist see how the anger between mother and father enables a son's chemical use by rendering the parents' united limit-setting impossible or ineffective; or how one parent's chemical dependence detaches him or her from the non-using spouse and children, resulting in their coalition against the using parent, which pushes the CD member farther away, and results in a tighter coalition of non-using parent and children. Systemically, this self-maintaining family cycle is all thrown in together—as complex, and as simple, as a bowl of spaghetti.

The interchanges and mutual reactions may seem difficult to understand, but within the systems framework we can make sense of it. The systems view provides some coherence and meaning to much of the self-defeating (and courageous) behaviors of CD families. It can assist us in choosing a general direction, a therapeutic road map to guide the family during its early recovery. Also, systems therapy gives us numerous techniques—our working tools—to do the job.

Many of the techniques and approaches in this book come from the Structural and Strategic Schools of family therapy, which are brief, systems-oriented, goal-directed models, which have been adapted to working with CD families. Many of the methods and techniques in this volume were created simply because they were needed. Some were discovered accidentally during family sessions, and others were garnered from the writings, workshops, or live observations of other professionals. Whatever their source, they have all been used in therapy with CD families. None of these techniques work magic (although Alter Ego—see Chapter 5—has come close a few times), but taken together, they make up a chorus of responses to the often asked question, "I see what's going on in this family, but what can I do about it?"

Most of the approaches in this book assume that the chemically dependent family member is part of a separate treatment program, either outpatient, inpatient and/or Alcoholics Anonymous or Narcotics Anonymous. If the CD member is not in a separate treatment program, getting him or her there becomes the first priority. The second priority, then, is to connect other family members to their own long-term support: Al-Anon, Naranon, Alateen, Families Anonymous, or other appropriate self-help group. Treating chemical dependence with family therapy alone is not advocated.

Likewise, neither is applying the same method to every family situation recommended. The upper-class parents who drag their adolescent son to therapy for one beer-drinking incident, and the angry, denying, court-ordered man and his family who come to treatment after his twenty-year history of alcoholism are not the same, and cannot be treated as if they were. In fact, there should be a warning label attached to a "how-to-do-it" book when the intricate skills of

psychotherapy are the subject. The warning on this label should say
something like this:

> People and families are too complex to reduce the art of therapy to
> a cookbook. The methods and techniques in this book are intended
> to serve as a guide only, not a firm set of procedures that apply to
> every family and every situation.

As therapists, we inevitably learn that nothing we have works for
everybody, and that everything we have works for somebody. The
trick is using the right approach at the right time with the family with
whom we're working. That trick, of course, is mastered only by
practice and experience—first, by mastering the fundamentals, then
by learning to use advanced interventions tailored to the specific
problem and family at hand. After working with hundreds of CD
families, I am convinced that no book or training workshop can
substitute for the essential task of putting in our hours in the therapy
room. Hands-on experience is the only way to get a feel for the work,
to learn from our mistakes, and to make interventions more fitting and
on target.

I am reminded of a wood craftsman who fashioned graceful and
sturdy furniture from natural materials using only a hatchet and a
shaving knife. The craftsman was asked how he did it. "Well, it ain't
that hard", he said, as he deftly chipped away at the wood. "You just
hit right where you're aimin', and the more you practice the luckier you
get."

Part One

Principles of the Family Systems Approach

Chapter 1

A Systems View of Chemically Dependent Families

The Systems Orientation to Families

This chapter lays a foundation for understanding the systems orientation to therapy for chemically dependent (CD) families. All the approaches and techniques in later chapters rest on this foundation. The intent of this clinical guidebook is to present practical techniques and ideas for face-to-face therapy with CD families. Since this is a practical, rather than a theoretical book, this section on systems theory is brief. For a more studied treatment of this interesting topic, the reader can explore the titles in the Bibliography at the end of this book. Especially recommended are *Foundations of Family Therapy* by Lynn Hoffman, an intriguing look at systems theory in family therapy, and *Lives of a Cell* by Lewis Thomas, an entertaining reading on systems thinking in the biological sciences.

All human groups, including families, have four major characteristics:

1. *Organization:* role and task assignments that divide functions of the system among its elements.
2. *Interaction:* communication among the elements to achieve the purpose of the group.

3. *Interdependence:* mutuality of influence; action by one part affects one or more other parts; the elements do not operate independently.
4. *Stability:* balance and predictability over time; the tendency to remain the same until internal or external pressures require a change.

These four characteristics of systems are useful to keep in mind when working with families.

Organization is necessary to conduct the business of being a family: providing emotional and economic security to its members, and preparing children for independent living in society. All families have some organization, even those who seem to be in chaos. Without a degree of organization, and with no role differentiation between members, the group would be a collection of individuals, not a family.

Some form of *interaction* occurs between and among members. Even in those families whose members appear to be detached and distant from each other, communication occurs, including the agreement not to communicate. For the purpose of conducting family therapy, it is reasonable to assume that the family is important to each member for a variety of emotional, social, and economic reasons.

The third characteristic, *interdependence*, is the key to understanding systems thinking. Interdependence implies mutual action-reaction, a circular pattern of cause and effect. For example, when the daughter gets angry, mother gets angry at the daughter, which results in the daughter's frustrated silence, leading to less (or greater) anger by the mother. Each person's action prompts a reaction, which changes the action, thus changing the reaction. Members' behaviors are mutually dependent.

Stability is an odd idea to a therapist working with a family that is in constant flux and chaos and that exhibits seemingly unstable, random and crisis-oriented behavior. But a deeper look will reveal a consistency in the family's ups and downs, a pattern of sorts. Attempts to change such an "unstable" family will reveal how stable it actually is.

8

Stability helps to explain the bugaboo of all therapists—resistance. Much of what we define as resistance is the family's attempt to maintain balance, familiar patterns, and other features of an organized social unit. Families will resist outside influences, including therapists, because the new input feels unfamiliar and awkward; it's not their accustomed way of doing things.

Systems vs. Individual Orientation

The systems approach to CD family therapy places primary emphasis on the relationships among members, rather than on the individual dynamics of each member. The statement "He or she never listens to what I say" can be understood several different ways. The individually-oriented therapist hears the statement as an expression about how an individual feels (angry). The systems-oriented therapist hears it more as a statement about a relationship between two people ("Our communication does not work"). When a spouse says, "My spouse drinks too much," the individually-oriented therapist may hear a statement about a person's drinking habits, or that one person is upset about the drinking behavior of another person. The systems-oriented therapist hears this, too, but also hears that a *relationship* is in conflict over the drinking issue. When a child says to a parent, "If you would just treat me more like Mom/Dad does," the individually-oriented therapist hears the child's frustration and anger toward one parent. The systems-oriented therapist hears this and also hears that a *relationship* triangle may exist between the child and parents, or hears more indirectly about the conflicting *relationship* between the two parents, who may disagree on how to treat the child.

Whereas an individual orientation toward therapy highlights the feelings, thoughts, and behavior of the individual person, the systems orientation highlights family patterns or repetitive sequences of actions and reactions between members. Consider an example of a conversation between a mother, father, and teenage daughter who were in therapy for the daughter's marijuana and alcohol dependence. The following is an interaction between family members about the daughter breaking curfew:

> *Father* (to mother): You didn't say anything to her when she came in an hour late last night.
>
> *Mother*: Well, you were so mad I was afraid to say anything.
>
> *Father*: Of course I was mad! Couldn't you see that she was testing us?
>
> *Mother*: I could see that you were all over her with anger and that she was hurt.
>
> *Daughter* (to father): I *told* you my friend's car broke down.
>
> *Father* (to mother): If you believe *that* you're a pushover.
>
> *Mother*: I wanted to hear about her friend's car breaking down, but you wouldn't let her talk.
>
> *Father*: We've heard the car story before.
>
> *Daughter*: My God! Am I supposed to know how to fix the car?

The above sequence ended in frustrated silence. As the father attacked the daughter, the mother protected her; this made him more angry at both the daughter and the mother. Also, the parents reacted to *each other* as much as they reacted to the daughter and the problem at hand. Each person acted and reacted; each responded to the others in an interlocking spiral, leading to a predictable outcome.

An individual orientation concentrates on each person's behavior, feelings, and communications as they are expressed to the therapist. The dialogue flow is mostly between the family member and the therapist. In the above dialogue about curfew, an individually-oriented therapist who is seeing the family together may have asked each person to relate his or her interpretation of the incident and his or her individual feelings about the incident. But in such an exchange between the therapist and one member, the therapist could easily miss the mother-father battle embedded in the father-daughter battle. If the family "enacts" the incident, talking to one another, rather than reporting to the therapist, the underlying patterns between and among the members is much clearer.

A systems-oriented therapist wants to observe the family communication patterns unfold—not only hear them described but also see them happen. When members interact with one another, a different level of information, an entirely new dimension is added. It's the difference between *being told* about how two or more people interacted and *observing* the interaction firsthand. The following diagrams distinguish these two types of communication between the therapist and family.

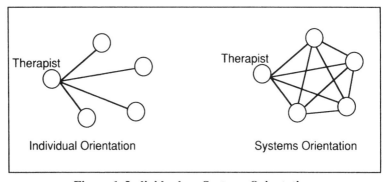

Figure 1. Individual vs. Systems Orientation

In Figure 1, the circles represent family members in a therapy dialogue, and the lines between the circles represent verbal and nonverbal communication and dialogue. In the individual orientation, the therapist remains central to the communication flow, focusing on his or her interaction with each member, one at a time. In the systems orientation, the focus broadens to include the interaction *between* members and the members' reactions to dialogue between other members.

To compare the non-systemic (individual) and systemic orientations by the therapist, the following tables separate the two approaches into two discrete categories. In the left column the therapist is primarily interested in what occurs *within* an individual in the family session. In the right column the therapist is interested in both what occurs within an individual and between individual members.

**Examples of
Questions Asked by the Therapist**

Non-Systemic Questions	**Systemic Questions**
(to son): How do you feel when there are arguments in the family?	(to son): Would you tell your parents how you feel when they get angry at your sister for being late?
(to wife): How do you feel when you and your husband have open disagreements about this?	(to wife): When you and your husband have open disagreements, who reacts the most, your son or your daughter?
(to one parent): What will happen if your son continues to use alcohol and marijuana?	(to both parents): Together, can you decide what you will do if your son continues his use of drugs?
(to son): How did you feel when your parents restricted you for the weekend?	(to daughter): What did your brother do when your parents told him he was restricted for the weekend?
(To father and son): When you have a disagreement, what happens?	(to mother): What do you do when your husband and son have a disagreement?

Examples of
Therapist Process

Non-Systemic Process	Systemic Process
Stays central—the "switchboard" for family communication in the room.	Allows and encourages members to talk to each other.
Elicits feelings from a member while the family listens.	Gently directs a member to ". . . tell him/her how you feel."
Is easily "captured" by the most verbal member.	Brings others into the conversation between the therapist and verbal member.
Watches only the person talking.	Notices reactions of all members when one is talking.
Does not allow interruptions when talking to one member.	Gains information about family relationships from interruptions.
Focuses on individual members, one at a time.	Comments on relationships between members.

Examples of
Thinking ("Self-Talk") by the Therapist

Non-Systemic Thinking	Systemic Thinking
When the husband and wife talk, he dominates the conversation.	They are cooperating in a pattern where he talks more than she does.
She is passive.	The more she follows, the more he leads, and the more he leads, the more she follows.
He is aggressive.	The more she gives in to him, the more firmly he attacks.
The mother is too strict with the children.	The mother is strict to the degree the father is lenient.
The father is too protective of the children.	The father is protective of the children to the degree the mother is firm in her discipline.
The teenager is controlling the family.	When mother and father disagree about how to react to the teenager, the teenager is in charge.
The father is withdrawn and detached from the family.	The father withdraws to the degree the mother and children are close.
The mother is overinvolved with the children.	The mother is involved with the children to the extent the father is withdrawn from the family.

All of the therapist's questions and actions need not have a systems focus. Some questions are asked to obtain specific information and are not intended to elicit family patterns ("How long has the problem existed?" "When did that happen?"). Other actions by the therapist serve to manage the session: maintaining benevolent control in the interview; bringing silent members into the conversation; discovering an individual's present feelings and thoughts; encouraging each member's participation.

Systems thinking operates in the background of the therapist's mind as he or she conducts the session and makes moment-to-moment decisions about what to do or say. The systems orientation shapes the therapist's actions with families and helps broaden their view of the problem to include everyone as part of the solution.

If the therapist thinks and acts systemically, the family gets the picture without the therapist having to make an issue of it. In fact, this approach is more likely to affect the family on an out-of-awareness level than on a conscious, intellectual one. While attending to the family's immediate emotional needs, the therapist's repetitive actions and language speak the systems message.

The systems therapist is manager and director of the session— sometimes focusing on an individual, sometimes spotlighting the interaction between two or three members, sometimes stepping back to see the family as a whole. To keep a balanced view and to understand the family dance, the therapist-as-director is always viewing a set of *relationships*, not a collection of individuals acting independently.

At first, the systems orientation to therapy does not feel natural to most therapists trained in individual counseling. When they attempt to shift to a family orientation, many hold on to the familiar and comfortable one-on-one approach. Rather than work interactionally and systemically, they are more inclined toward individual therapy during family sessions. Initially, they are not aware of doing this, and most are surprised by a supervisor-therapist dialogue like the following which could take place after a session:

Supervisor:	That was a long and powerful interaction between you and the wife during the session.
Therapist:	Was it ever! I'm drained.
Supervisor:	Maybe you're working too hard.
Therapist:	I feel like it at times.
Supervisor:	Then try sharing the work with her husband. Maybe you could help the couple have the same intense experience you had with the wife.
Therapist:	What's wrong with the way I did it?
Supervisor:	The question is not what is right or wrong but what is more effective in moving the couple to a new level of communication. Who needs to learn to explore the wife's feelings and thoughts the way you did so effectively?
Therapist:	The husband, I guess.
Supervisor:	Good.

Systemic therapists use their range and flexibility. Sometimes the therapist acts as the central switchboard. At other times, however, he or she allows the family to do its own work by encouraging family members to talk to one another on topics important to them. While the latter is happening, the systemic therapist supports, comments, clarifies, focuses, respectfully challenges, brings other members into the conversation, or, when appropriate, prevents others from interfering. Richer exploration and discoveries are possible when the family is allowed to experience itself through guided interaction.

Chemically Dependent Families as Systems

Most families don't think systemically about themselves. Rather, they focus on the individual level. And when they have a problem, they usually present it on the individual level. Families generally are unable to see that their family patterns make up an equation and that individual members contribute to it in varying degrees.

Families that have the problem of one or more chemically dependent members develop certain interactional patterns to manage and survive the problem. When a parent is the chemically dependent member, a common pattern is for the non-using spouse to become closer to the children as a way of protecting them from the dependent member's influence. Another common pattern is for fights or silent conflicts between mother and father to result in the siblings drawing closer together and, depending on their relative ages, even forming a coalition against the chemically dependent, or against both parents.

The two patterns mentioned above are normal reactions to the disease of chemical dependence in a family. Predictably, and in order to survive, the family adjusts to the disease. This adjustment, however, results in an unhealthy family structure and a pervasive emotional pollution from which there seems to be no escape.

Often, a family adjusts so thoroughly to the chemical dependence that it becomes as much a part of its environment as the air they breathe, and the family fails to see the true impact of the disease on them as a family. If a parent is the dependent member, the alcohol or other drug use can be embedded as a family ritual and included in its schedule of activities, becoming the "reality" that the family members, especially the children, have known all their lives. If the family remains intact, members learn to manage in spite of the problem, and as time goes by, abnormal family life becomes the norm. Rigid and unhealthy relationship patterns—coalitions against the user, conflicts and violence, inappropriate closeness or distance between certain members, co-dependence and enabling—become the status quo.

When viewed systemically, the family is seen as an element in a larger system—a piece of its extended family, its neighborhood, its cultural surroundings. Of course, the complete system or social context is never present during therapy. This requires the therapist to be mindful that forces outside the home, such as extended family, peers, neighborhood, other professionals, and living conditions can make important contributions to family dynamics and to the problem presented for treatment.

Advantages of Working Systemically

The systems approach with chemically dependent families has practical advantages during therapy:

1. It helps us understand why people act the way they do. For example, a young person's excessive shyness or aggression often makes no sense when seen in the school or peer context, but the origin of these behaviors might become clearer when viewed within the family context.

2. Thinking systemically forces the therapist to think in complementary patterns. For example, to the degree that one parent and child are overinvolved (enmeshed), the other parent and same child may be distant or in conflict with one another.

3. The systems orientation reminds us that change in one part of the system affects the whole. For example, when a child's behavior improves, a mother's anger toward the father could decrease. Or, when the conflict between father and child eases, the relationship between that child and a sibling could improve.

4. It helps us to understand resistance, and therefore, to tolerate it better. What we interpret as resistance may be the family's normal pattern. For example, a father may resist the therapist's request to have a conversation with his son about the son's school work because in this family the mother usually deals directly with the son on this issue; the father's input is typically through the mother.

5. Thinking systemically erases the notion of blame, at least

theoretically. For example, a teenager often becomes uncommunicative when questioned by a parent about his or her activities, feelings, and thoughts. This can lead to a frustrating dialogue—the more the parent questions, the less information the teenager gives. Both members are justified in their behavior: the teenager won't give the parent information because he or she experiences the parent's questions as intrusive and prying; but the parent has to be inquisitive because the teenager won't volunteer information about himself or herself. Each one is acting reasonably in this context. Who is to blame?

6. The systems orientation reminds us to think of the problem behavior within the broader context of family, extended family, peers, neighborhood, and other professional helpers. The individual and his or her nuclear family are only part of a larger social and cultural environment.

Because systems therapy for chemical dependence has a broader view of the social and relationship context for the problem, it has more power and more flexibility than the individual orientation to treatment. It has more power because significant influences, other than that of the therapist, motivate the CD family member toward recovery. The therapist's influence on the recovering member, although important, is more superficial and temporary; the family's or significant other's influence is more intense and lasting.

The systems approach has more flexibility than an individual orientation because in individual counseling and therapy, the communication possibilities—who talks to whom—are limited to two (therapist to client or client to therapist). When even one family member is present with the client and therapist, the who-talks-to-whom options are increased to six. These increased options add significant flexibility for the therapist, especially when he or she views all these possibilities within a systems framework.

If systems concepts are valuable, why not simply educate families about systems so that they will understand themselves? Because directly educating families about systems during therapy sessions is like interrupting an argument between two people to explain the dynamics of their fight; they may stop briefly, but they are quickly pulled back into the fray. Emotional triggers are more powerful than logical explanation. It's best to work systemically with the family while attending to its immediate needs and concerns. This will help members experience a family problem as an interactional, as well as an individual, process.

Characteristics of This Approach

The therapy model described in this book is adapted from the Structural and Strategic Schools of family therapy.* It is a brief, goal-directed, systems-oriented approach requiring active interventions by the therapist.

To say that this approach is a "brief" model means that it is designed to accomplish certain worthwhile goals within five to ten one-hour family sessions. Therapy is based on getting into the family quickly, working with several limited goals, and then disengaging.

A brief model has advantages over a longer term approach. CD families are much more likely to enter and remain in brief therapy than in more extended treatment. It is also a more economical use of staff time; a brief approach allows more clients to be treated.

Of course, a brief model also has some disadvantages. Family recovery is a long-term, not a short-term, process. The intention of this model is to get the family started, to help the family during primary treatment of the CD member and during his or her early sobriety, and to urge the family toward long-term support for its continuing recovery (through AA, NA, Al-Anon, Naranon, and other twelve-step programs, or co-dependence treatment). Family members are encouraged to return later for an occasional follow-up or crisis family session if needed. A second disadvantage of brief therapy is that it does not go

---

* In the Bibliography, several references contain detailed information about this School of family therapy, especially the books by Minuchin, Haley, Stanton, and others.

into the clinical depth some therapists prefer; it is a problem-solving approach, not an in-depth, analytic growth model.

Saying that this therapy approach is "goal-directed" refers to certain realistic goals for the short duration of the therapy. Goals are systems-focused, limited, and achievable. The five primary goals of therapy will be discussed in the next chapter.

Describing the approach as "systems-oriented" refers to a dynamic, interactional view of the relationships in a family. The systems orientation, however, is more than a guiding set of theoretical assumptions—it is an applied method in therapist-family encounters. When the therapist asks family members to talk to each other instead of to the therapist, or gently comments on the repeated intrusions of an enmeshed, enabling father during a mother-son dialogue, or asks a mother and father to hold hands to symbolize unified parenting for their chemically dependent teenager, the therapist is applying a systems orientation to the therapy.

Finally, saying that the approach requires the therapist to make "active interventions" refers to the directives the therapist needs to give. With appropriate respect and timing, the therapist actually *tells* family members what to do: "Talk together now about . . ." "Let's you and I sit here and listen to your wife and daughter talk about . . ." "Decide together now what you will do if . . ." "Tell your son something he hasn't heard you say before . . ."

At first, telling people what to do in therapy might seem appalling to some therapists, especially those trained in Rogerian non-directive therapy or something similar. Family members, however, don't mind being told what to do if the directives are given with respect, energy, optimism, and sometimes humor, and if they are relevant to their concerns.

The therapist must give directives that are designed to encourage the family members to experience a broader range of behavior with each other. This therapy approach emphasizes the experiential aspects of change: if a recovering father, for example, can have an understanding, compassionate talk with his child in the session, instead of the

21

customary "do-right" lecture, everyone will experience something different. Brief therapy requires the therapist to be directive, with gentle skill, patience, and a genuine understanding of how difficult—and how possible—family change can be.

The systems approach to therapy assumes that all behavior doesn't originate from within the individual, but is triggered and maintained by the patterns—the repetitious interactions—between and among the members of the family. The total of the family system is greater than the sum of its individual elements. The family interaction and the integrity of the organization adds a new dimension to the individual behaviors of the members which comprise the system. In CD treatment, the dependence process itself is the most immediate cause of the alcohol or other drug use; a more distant cause is the dysfunctional family situation. A chemically dependent person uses alcohol or other drugs because of his or her craving for the drug, not because he or she is a member of a dysfunctional family. However, being a member of a dysfunctional family can contribute to the alcohol or other drug use by making it more urgent for one or more members to seek escape, relief from tension, and medication for various negative feelings. And most important, the family dysfunction, although not directly causing the CD, can contribute quite directly to preventing recovery. The family may not be a direct cause of the problem, but it can be a direct cause for preventing a solution.

When a CD family member enters treatment, the systems-oriented therapist wants to know about his or her family relationships. Including family members in the CD member's treatment can accomplish three things: (1) motivate the CD member for recovery; (2) help to make the family more supportive to the recovering member; and (3) help to engage the family itself in a recovery program. If the CD member is in treatment and remains abstinent, but the family remains dysfunctional and without treatment, the chances of the CD member's recovery are jeopardized, and the chances for the other family members' recoveries are nonexistent.

Procedures for Family Therapy Assumed in this Book

The procedures for conducting family therapy will differ according to the setting of the CD family member's treatment—outpatient or inpatient—and that treatment's length. For the purposes of the family systems approach to therapy described in this book, the following procedures are assumed:

1. The identified patient (IP) has been referred to an inpatient or outpatient center for treatment for chemical dependence.
2. The center has a family component in its treatment program. At the time the IP calls for an appointment, or during the assessment interview with the IP, he or she is invited to bring his or her family ("everyone living in the home") to the center for the family component of treatment. Depending on the center, a variety of family activities may be offered, including weekly family education groups on the disease concept of CD, as well as related information, discussion and films for family members, Al-Anon or Naranon meetings in the center, multiple family groups, and/or children's activity and education groups. Depending on the nature of the activity and the preferences of the treatment center, the IP may or may not be present during these sessions.
3. Included as part of the family component are conjoint family sessions with one family consisting of the IP and all of his or her family members who will attend. In outpatient treatment these single family sessions are usually held weekly, beginning within one to three weeks after the IP has entered the treatment center. These single family sessions are normally about an hour in length and continue for five to ten sessions, depending on the length of the IP's treatment. If aftercare treatment for families is available at the center, a family may receive more than ten sessions.

4. Inpatient centers that serve families that live out of the area usually have a "family week" program of three to five consecutive days during which the out-of-town family members, who may reside in a local motel, attend various forms of educational and therapy groups, including conjoint sessions with the IP.

5. In either outpatient or inpatient treatment, the conjoint family sessions are conducted by staff members of the family component at the treatment center. These family counselors might also conduct the family education and orientation sessions, multiple family groups, children's groups, or other family activities.

6. The family counselor is usually responsible for recruiting the IP's family for treatment, and is either contacted by the intake worker concerning whom to invite for the family component, or, in some centers, the family counselor is part of the intake session if a member of the IP's family attends this session. This is the family counselor's chance to hear the family members' stories and to recruit the remaining members for the family component of the treatment center.

Chapter 2

Goals for Therapy

What are we trying to accomplish with brief family therapy for chemical dependence when the IP (or CD client) is in treatment and is, at least for now, sober and drug-free?

This chapter presents and discusses five general goals for the systems model for treating chemically dependent families. Chapters 3-6 offer practical suggestions that address these goals:

1. To increase motivation for recovery
2. To convey the whole-family-message
3. To change family patterns that work against recovery
4. To prepare the family for what to expect in early recovery
5. To encourage family members' own long-term support

GOAL # 1: *To Increase Motivation for Recovery*

When the pain and anxiety caused by chemical dependence or other compulsive behavior become greater than the pain of changing, a person or a family is motivated. Of course, this assumes that people are aware of the connection between the chemical dependence and the emotional pain and anxiety they feel. Family sessions can help them make this connection.

When I began learning family therapy for CD problems, I was doing mostly individual and group therapy in a chemical dependence treatment center. Family therapy was entirely new to me, and in those early months I remember making two observations relating to recovery motivation and family therapy.

First, I observed that the family member who was under the most emotional stress was usually not the IP; it was a spouse, parent, or child. A family member was usually the first to cry, the first to admit to psychosomatic complaints, and the first to become highly emotional in the session. It seemed that CD problems were harder on the family than on the CD member. This surprised me; I thought the one suffering the most had to be the IP. After all, he or she was the one in treatment.

Likewise, I was surprised to discover that the family member who was the most "sick and tired of being sick and tired" and the most motivated to relieve his or her pain was frequently not the IP. It was the long-suffering spouse or parent of the CD family member. This observation is commonplace now, but then it was a revelation.

Thirdly, I discovered that the IP became more nervous during family sessions than during other therapies in our inpatient program. In individual therapy, clients were often relatively relaxed, chatty, responsive, and seemed to enjoy the conversation. The IPs in group therapy acted generally the same way once they became accustomed to the setting. But several days before an IP's family arrived for its scheduled appointment I saw anxiety in the IP that I had not seen before. The closer the appointment time for the session, the more nervous the IP became, asking questions about the time for the session or about who would be present; it was obviously on the IP's mind. When the big day arrived, the IP was not as relaxed, talkative or witty in the family interview as in group or individual sessions. He or she was more serious and intense.

This discovery surprised me, since I had assumed that the IP would be more comfortable with his or her family than with relative strangers. But I was wrong. Experience has shown that IPs are more anxious in therapy with their families than they are in therapy with strangers. Why? The painful feelings of guilt, anger and shame have occurred mostly in the family context, and since their family represents their past and future, IPs have more to gain or lose than they have with just their counselors or peers in a group.

Fortunately, this anxiety caused by the family presence is beneficial—even necessary—for change. The family presence in therapy provides the needed anxiety and motivation for recovery in several ways. First, some IPs eventually realize that they will lose their family if they continue their alcohol or other drug use. This arouses fears of abandonment, loneliness, and loss of love. Secondly, the IP may be truly tired of the family quarrels and conflicts—the arguments, the blame and counter-blame, or the silent, oppressive tension. Thirdly, if the IP is a parent, he or she may suffer from guilt about his or her chemical dependence being harmful to the family, especially the children. The chronic pain of parental guilt is a strong motivator.

Children often have special motivating power in CD family therapy. I have repeatedly seen children, especially young ones, become the deciding influence on a chemically dependent parent or grandparent to enter treatment and begin abstinence and recovery. Every experienced therapist can recall the young child in a family session, who, with the innocence and sincerity only a child can manage, melts the angry facade of a mother, father, or grandparent. One such experience was a six-year-old girl who brought her denying alcoholic father to tears with, "Daddy, will you ever get well?" CD parents may not go into treatment for themselves, for their spouse, for their parents, or even for their job, financial security, or personal health, but a few will start a serious recovery effort for one or more children in the family.

Ultimately, of course, successful recovery depends on CD clients getting well for themselves, not for someone else. Nevertheless, the emotional leverage of children or grandchildren in pain can be a powerful motivation to start. The impact is more immediate and compelling if the younger children are present in some of the family sessions. When they are not present, the therapist should find an opportunity to mention each child by name in every session with parents. If children are not present and not mentioned, the therapist is unwittingly enabling the parents to deny the effects of the CD on their children. Family sessions also motivate the recovery of the non-CD members. Co-dependence, now receiving much well-deserved attention in the CD field, has its own set of rigid, compulsive, debilitating, and self-defeating behaviors. An enabler, like the CD family member, will frequently not change what he or she is doing (once realized) without the pain and guilt caused by what his or her behavior is doing to himself or herself and to the family. Often, enabling parents or spouses finally detach and stick to setting limits on the CD member, not for themselves, but to protect others in the family. Therapy sessions can raise the family's awareness of co-dependence and lead to a separate recovery program for the co-dependent person or persons.

Other compulsive behaviors such as eating disorders in one or more family members may surface during therapy. The stereotype of the slim alcoholic and the obese spouse is almost common enough to warrant the stereotype. The spouse's "bar" is the refrigerator, and his or her emotional refuge is food, which carries its own physical and emotional problems.

Anorexia and bulemia are increasingly common eating disorders which can be exposed during family interviews. They usually involve teenage girls and are prevalent in chemically dependent families, as well as in rigid families with the facade of super-normality or perfection. These disorders are life-threatening and should be referred to a qualified specialist whenever they are suspected.

Psychosomatic complaints by the spouse or parent of the CD member are also pulled to the surface in family sessions. These are so common, in fact, that therapists should routinely inquire about the health of the primary co-dependent and his or her "symptom list"— sleeping disorders, high blood pressure, chest pains, migraine headaches, gastrointestinal problems and nervous conditions. This list can be talked about in therapy sessions as a way of motivating the CD client. If a CD husband, for example, believes that his wife may physically or emotionally collapse under the strain, he pays more attention to her, knowing that if she falls, the whole family tent can come crashing down on his head.

Family sessions often expose and increase motivation for recovery, especially when the family realizes that the CD member's problem is actually the family's problem.

GOAL # 2: *To Convey the "Whole-Family-Message"*

As discussed in Goal #1, the entire family—not just the CD member—is affected by chemical dependence. As treatment professionals, we know this, and sometimes we naively assume that the family also knows it. However, families usually don't think in whole-family terms about chemical dependence. They see one person who has a drinking or other drug problem. This description from the wife of a middle-stage alcoholic is typical:

> My husband, Charlie, drinks too much. When he starts drinking there is usually trouble, but he doesn't admit that his drinking is the problem. He gets very angry when the children or I bring it up. He could cut back or stop if he really wanted to. It's good that he's coming to a treatment center for education and counseling so he won't drink like that or stop completely.

The interesting part about this description is that it is all about Charlie—the problem is located within one person. Obviously, this is not a whole-family view. Before entering treatment, family members usually don't recognize that if the problem is long-standing, the family is centered and organized around the alcohol or other drug use, that each family member has his or her own set of emotional, behavioral, school, or work problems, and that everyone is contributing his or her share to the family misery and vice versa, in a self-maintaining fashion.

The whole-family-message in therapy makes the link between the chemical dependence and the other family problems. Of course, the inevitable "chicken and egg" dilemma surfaces: Does the alcohol or

29

other drug use cause the family problems or do the family problems cause the drug use? This question is difficult to manage because it presumes an either/or answer. The therapist who thinks in systemic, interactional terms is not bound by the either/or dichotomy. This makes the answer easy: It's both. Alcohol or other drug use and family problems are both causes and effects of each other in a self-maintaining cycle.

This is not to imply that family problems are the cause of chemical dependence in one of its members. We don't know for certain what causes chemical dependence. No doubt it's a complex interplay of biological, psychological, and social factors. But once it starts, it maintains itself and usually progresses—sometimes with amazing speed, sometimes slowly over a period of years—until it debilitates the users and those around them.

For this reason, CD problems must be considered to be primary. The chemical dependence must be treated first. In multi-problem families, the practical reality is that the family tension and stress, whatever its origin and character, cannot be worked on while the alcohol or other drug use continues, because the chemical dependence keeps the system in emotional turmoil. The storm on the surface prevents resolution of other problems. By stopping the alcohol or other drug use, family tension will be positively affected to some degree. At the very least, family waters will be calmed long enough to explore family patterns—isolation, lack of communication, coalitions, and hidden or open conflict—that may be enabling or in some way maintaining the CD family cycle.

Family change frequently begins with the simple awareness of how the problem is affecting everyone in the family. When members begin to think in whole-family terms, they become more aware of why everyone acts the way they do and to make connections between the addiction and the other family problems. A CD teenager, for example, can maintain extreme tension in the home, especially between the parents. The open or hidden disagreements about how to handle the adolescent's problem can increase the distance and conflicts between parents, between the CD adolescent and one or both parents, and between other children in the home. The turmoil can push the children into their own psychological and emotional world and increase their absence from home and family. Some will begin to have school, social, or personal problems.

All this can be compounded into the "good child/bad child" family, in which the non-using, good child is under almost as much pressure to excel as the using, bad child is to change. A balancing act is created: to the degree one is bad, the other must be good, and vice versa. The glaring differences between the siblings inevitably sets up comparisons between the two, making matters worse. The message conveyed to the bad child becomes a self-fulfilling prophesy. The good child is pressured to be perfect, a formidable burden on a developing child. This non-problem child is easy for the parents (and therapist) to overlook during family recovery.

For some families, the CD child becomes a scapegoat, someone to blame for the family misery. This well-known phenomenon happens in families with many different presenting problems. In CD families, scapegoating is even more acute because the blame is focused on the specific and "voluntary" act of alcohol or other drug use: "If he or she didn't drink or use other drugs, the family would be fine." The scapegoat draws the attention away from other problematic relationships, thus protecting the family.

The whole-family-message is more of a by-product of family sessions than it is a direct therapeutic input. It is often conveyed indirectly, beginning with inviting everyone living in the home to the first interview. Even if the whole family doesn't show up, the therapist talks about the importance of getting the missing members to attend, thus making the point that chemical dependence is a family affair.

The whole-family-message is conveyed directly, however, when the therapist makes systemic statements in therapy: To parents: "How is your son affected when the two of you have an argument with your daughter about her drug use?" To a father: "Who reacts more strongly when you and your son have an argument, your wife, your other son, or your daughter?" Questioning family members about one another is an excellent technique for conveying the interactional nature of CD family patterns.

The whole-family-message is also conveyed when the therapist helps the family realize that CD is a disease. Family members often respond to the drinking or other drug-use behavior of a member according to what they believe about it. If family members think of chemical dependence as a moral issue, they react to the CD member's behavior as bad, depraved, and evil. If they view it as a defect of character, they see the CD member as someone showing weakness, personality disturbance, and deep-seated neurosis. If the treatment staff helps family members view CD as a disease, however, they can be helped to view the CD member as someone who is sick and in need of specific treatment for the successful management of the disease. Education can change the family's view, with consequent changes in the family's reactions.

Ideally, the family disease concept is best presented separately in family orientation or in education groups using lectures, films, and discussion periods, rather than in family therapy sessions. Education is such an important part of treatment for chemical dependence that it needs its own time and place.

GOAL # 3: *To Change Family Patterns That Work Against Recovery*

There are at least four family patterns that work against the long-term recovery of the family and the CD member: (1) enabling, (2) conflicts, (3) coalitions, and (4) the peripheral CD family member. Although there are other relationship patterns that can undermine recovery, these seem to be the most common. They are closely related, and the presence of one often indicates others. The goal during the family sessions is to address these patterns if they are present and to assist the family to discover alternatives. The following describes patterns and general goals of family therapy. Specific therapy strategies for these patterns are discussed in Chapters 3 and 7.

Enabling

Most family members who have enabled a loved one to avoid the consequences of his or her alcohol or other drug use are doing the best they can to help. What CD professionals call enabling, they call love, concern, fulfilling obligations, and protecting the family. When a wife makes excuses for her alcoholic husband, she may be indirectly enabling his alcohol use, but she is also protecting herself, her children, the family image in the community, and possibly the family's financial security. Safety and family preservation are usually her immediate intentions.

"Enable" means to make able; to provide with means or opportunity; to make possible. Some family members, when told they are enabling, hear the therapist implying that they have an active and direct responsibility for maintaining the disease or even causing it. This can create defensiveness and resistance. Thus, the therapist is usually wise to avoid using the "enabling" label early in family treatment. "Enabling" fails to recognize family members' intentions of helping, protecting, and ensuring family survival. It's better not to get into a semantics game with families and create resistance by using labels, especially in the early sessions. Later in therapy, or through family orientation and educating sessions, or in the firm and caring hands of Al-Anon or other self-help groups, families will come to understand the concept of enabling.

There is another innocent but troublesome word that can cause problems in working with enabling parent-child situations. The word is "helping." Urging parents "not to help their child so much" makes no sense to them. Therapists need to stay with the word "helping," but try to give it a new meaning. Here are some re-labeled definitions therapists can use in enmeshed, enabling family situations.

"Helping" children is:
—Allowing them to learn from natural consequences.
—Teaching them responsibility for their own actions.
—Giving them strong incentive to change.
—Loving them enough to let them skin their knees.
—Preparing them for the time when the parents will be gone.

A further problem with enabling patterns has to do with their endurance and resilience. Even when the active chemical use has stopped, enabling still threatens the family. A relapse of the CD member can trigger a relapse of the enabler and return the family to active drinking or other drug use. (Enabler: "He hasn't drunk in over two months; this one time won't hurt."). With a chemically dependent adolescent client, one or both parents can also passively enable a return to alcohol or other drug use by not knowing or not checking on the whereabouts and activities of the teenager. A spouse can enable his or her partner's occasional "slips" by reacting with old habits and failing to react with new behavior. If this should continue, neither will recover from his or her compulsion—both have just changed its frequency— and in a short time, the CD problem is likely to return to the pre-treatment state.

Enabling is a fundamental dynamic in some relationships and is not limited to enabling the use of alcohol or other drugs. Parents, for example, can allow or enable a recovering teenager to dominate the household with his or her moods, irresponsibility, or dangerous behavior. The alcohol or other drug use stops, but the enabling of disruptive behavior continues.

In some spouse or lover relationships the balance in the relation-ship is established around enabling. With one live-in couple I was seeing, the man's legal trouble from drug use forced him to abstain temporarily, but the enabling relationship with his girlfriend continued essentially unchanged. She supported him in her house, acted as his maid and cook, took his verbal and emotional abuse, allowed him the use of her car, and even gave him spending money. After hearing the details of this arrangement for several sessions, I finally asked her the inevitable question: "Why do you stay in this relationship?" Her sad reply told me how difficult a question that is for a co-dependent: "Well, sometimes after supper he helps me wash the dishes."

When co-dependents begin recovery through treatment or twelve-step group, they will understand enabling the way professionals do, and see how it applies throughout their relationships. Twelve-step groups provide more than increased awareness, education, labels, and good advice. They also offer continuing support, understanding, and the all-important influence of others who are successfully changing themselves.

Coalitions

A coalition exists when two or more family members unite against a third. A common example is that of a parent and one or more children united against the other parent. Coalitions can also include extended family members such as grandmother and father against mother, or one spouse and his or her sibling or close friend against the other spouse. For survival during active chemical use, family members often form coalitions against the CD member.

Coalitions, like enabling, may continue after sobriety. Since the non-CD parent and the children have often been much closer than the CD parent and children for the entire history of the family, we cannot expect such an ingrained pattern to change automatically when the CD parent gets sober. It takes time to adjust. Coalition patterns start changing when trust begins to be reestablished. Once the spouse and children start trusting the recovering parent to remain free of chemicals, and the spouse begins to trust his or her partner to have a closer emotional relationship with the children, the rigid pattern begins to loosen. Depending on the family history and the previous-use pattern of the CD member, this loosening could take several months to a year of sobriety. As a beginning, however, the therapist can create conversations between the recovering parent and children to make the point that the parent needs to to reestablish contact and trust with them.

Conflicts

Conflicts and coalitions are dynamically related—one has a direct effect on the other. The closeness of some relationships in a family can cause jealousy and resentment in other members; this spawns conflicts, which, in turn, tightens any existing coalitions. The recovering parent, for example, could be resentful and frustrated by the close relationship between the other parent and children. The recovering parent's lack of authority and influence in the home escalates his or her anger, resulting in a tighter protective bond between the non-CD parent and children. Or, in another situation, two siblings could form a coalition for mutual support during the parent's active chemical use and could remain that way even when the chemical use stops. At the same time, other children may resent this closeness, causing bickering, jealousy, and a strengthening of the bond between the close siblings.

Surprisingly, conflicts sometimes become worse during early sobriety than they were during the active chemical use. It is common to hear a spouse lament, "My husband doesn't drink any more, but things are no better in our family." Frequent conflicts after sobriety are dismaying, but the reasons they happen are understandable. The family buried some of its anger during the active chemical use to avoid conflicts and potentially dangerous clashes. During recovery, this submerged anger can pop to the surface, often at unexpected moments. I have seen parents suppress their anger toward each other until their chemically dependent adolescent was out of immediate danger, then let it fly during sessions, just at the time when they appeared to be united and achieving success in helping their child. I have also found recovering single parents to be surprised that their children not only failed to welcome their new sobriety with open arms, but got into trouble at school and became unmanageable at home after the parent had been drug free for several weeks. In recovering families, children often cannot acknowledge, or even identify, their feelings of anger, resentment, and constant fear of the parent's relapse, so they act out their negative emotions.

Also, when the recovering member becomes drug free, he or she may be more involved with the family on a day-to-day basis, creating more opportunities for conflict. The recovering person becomes clear headed, less guilty, and more assertive toward other family members. This especially applies if it is a parent who is recovering and starts taking more responsibility toward parenting, finances, and family activities. This new role may not be initially welcomed by the spouse, children, or the extended family. Resistance to change, even desirable change, is built into a family system.*

Peripheral CD Family Member

During active chemical use, a CD family member may set himself or herself apart from the family by psychologically distancing or emotionally isolating himself or herself to avoid conflict, or by forming a tight bond with his or her peer group of users. This is especially true of recovering teenagers who have identified with another peer culture, favoring music, language, clothes, and activities that are usually different from those of their siblings and certainly different from those of their parents. Similarly, a recovering single parent who had relinquished part of the parenting responsibilities to another person during his or her active chemical use can remain on the periphery after becoming free of chemicals. He or she can continue his or her isolation from the children, who by this time have become emotionally withdrawn to avoid the pain of depending on the CD parent. If the recovering single parent remains peripheral for too long, the remaining family can stabilize without him or her and can strongly resist the recovering

---

* For more information read *Healing the Hurt: Rebuilding Relationships with Your Children, A Self-Help Guide for Recovering Parents*, by Rosalie Cruise Jesse, Ph.D. (Minneapolis: Johnson Institute, 1990).

person's attempts at re-entering the family as a parent.

Continued isolation of a peripheral member works against family recovery. The recovering CD member may not feel needed in the family; everyone seems to function well without his or her presence. Feelings of not being essential to the family can add to the CD member's anger, resentment, and loneliness, leading to a relapse.

The goal of the therapist is to help the family adjust to the re-entry of the CD member into role-appropriate membership in the family. How quickly this is accomplished will vary, and it's important that families feel in control of the pace at which they adjust to the new role of the recovering member. The family's objective, however, must be to return to normal role expectations as rapidly as it can, without adding undue stress to its members.

GOAL # 4: *To Prepare the Family for What to Expect in Early Recovery*

Family members' expectations about early recovery are often unrealistic. This stems from one of the family myths about CD: "When the alcohol or other drug use stops, so do the problems." To be sure, many of the problems are eliminated: the CD member is usually less absent from the family; the physical and health dangers of chemical use cease; many of the arguments and fights during periods of heavy use stops; legal trouble is not a constant threat, and the financial drain caused by chemical dependence disappears. These blessed reliefs give many families justifiable cause for hope.

Still, families are likely to encounter a few unanticipated obstacles in the first year of recovery. The therapeutic goal here is to raise the family's awareness about what adjustment reactions and setbacks to expect. The therapeutic assumption is that being informed that a crisis may occur is less unsettling to families than to have a crisis popping up out of nowhere.

Although families react to recovery in unique ways, therapists can predict some of the following common family reactions during the first weeks or months of recovery:

1. An unexpected amount of anger and open conflict.
2. Mood swings of the recovering member as he or she adjusts to being free of alcohol or other drugs.
3. Arguments around mistrusting the CD member.
4. "Walking on egg shells" by the family to keep from upsetting the recovering member.
5. The CD member's withdrawal into a self-help program or other activity.
6. In the case of a CD parent, more disagreements between the parents about child management.
7. Relapses.

Chapter 7 will provide more detail on the topic of what families should expect in early recovery, especially as regards suggested strategies to deal with each of the above early roadblocks to recovery.

Although not all of these roadblocks will occur in every case, every family should be prepared to experience at least some of them. Each can be introduced by the therapist at appropriate places in the therapy sessions as being normal reactions of other families in similar situations. Most families aren't motivated to plan for all of these possibilities because they don't believe that they will happen to *them.* That is why the therapist should mention them as being normal— common reactions in a typical recovering family that do not indicate that the family is in deep trouble or hopeless. Then, should these crises occur, the family will recall their being mentioned and recognize their occurrence as something to be expected.

GOAL # 5: *To Encourage Family Members'*
Long-Term Support

As mentioned before, a short-term model is not designed for long-term support. Recovery for the family and the CD member begins with treatment, but contrary to the beliefs of some families, it doesn't end there. The chemical hangovers may be gone, but the emotional hangovers—anger, fear, low self-esteem, intimacy problems, and other complications—can linger well into sobriety. Thus, family members need to look at themselves, start taking responsibility for their own behavior, and begin to work their separate emotional and spiritual recovery programs. As therapists, we can refer, urge, encourage, cajole, wheedle, and coax, but we can't make family members go to self-help meetings. Almost always it's the family member who needs a self-help group the most who is the most resistant to going. That's why therapists must continue to refer, urge, encourage, cajole, wheedle, and coax.

In the matter of referrals, a sort of formula seems to apply: the greater the geographical distance between the treatment center and the self-help group meeting, the less likely that family members will go. A treatment center that has self-help meetings in its facility will, therefore, have greater success in connecting family members to long-term support groups than will a center without this internal resource.

Therapists need to tell families that in most large communities there is no shortage of recovery groups, most of which are based on the AA twelve-step philosophy. Likewise, Al-Anon has regular meetings in most communities that have AA meetings. Any family member or friend of someone who has an alcohol problem is welcome. Naranon, not yet nearly as widespread, is the counterpart for anyone involved with someone with a drug problem other than alcohol. Alateen is a self-help group for teenagers from families with a CD problem. Families Anonymous is for the parents of chemically dependent children. Tough Love meetings are made up of parents who are learning to apply firm, limit-setting contracts with their child around his or her chemical use and other behaviors. Adult Children of Alcoholics (ACOA) welcomes anyone whose life has been affected by parental chemical use. Relationships Anonymous (RA) and Co-dependents Anonymous (CODA) are self-help groups for people who have difficulties with their dependence on relationships with others, usually opposite-sexed partners.

In addition to giving family members information about local self-help meetings, therapists should see to it that appropriate booklets and pamphlets on chemical dependence are made available to the family at the first session (see pages 221-222 for a list of Johnson Institute booklets.) Some families utilize these quite well; others ignore them. Since we never know at the outset which families are which, it's best to provide them to everyone. Crisis intervention hotlines and emergency numbers should be given to every violence-prone family in treatment. We never know when the information will be needed and used by one or more family members.

~~~~~~

The five general therapy goals outlined in this chapter not only give the therapy purpose and direction but also give therapists a framework to evaluate recovery progress. The goals offer a clinical direction through an overlapping sequence of steps: motivate the family for recovery (Goal #1); let the family see that CD is a total family problem (Goal #2); point the family toward solutions to patterns and relationships that could result in leading the family to relapse (Goal #3); prepare family members for what to expect as a recovering family (Goal #4); and finally, hook family members into longer-term sources of support (Goal #5).

That's a lot to accomplish in five to ten one-hour sessions, true. But, by keeping the five goals in mind, the therapist will find that the therapy will be better focused and more organized. And a focused and organized therapy reduces the confusion and frustration of family members and therapists alike.

Part Two

Tools and Techniques of
the Systems Approach to Therapy

Chapter 3

Mapping Common Patterns in Chemically Dependent Families

Mapping is the technique of using symbols to draw the therapist's impressions of the family structure. It is a picture of the current family relationships—who has the apparent power, who is close or distant, who is aligned with whom, and who is in conflict with whom. It is distinguished from a family genogram in that a map is not always multi-generational, it does not contain social history, and it adds more information than a genogram about relationships between members. A map is a current and subjective picture of the emotional relationships between and among family members.

I borrowed this technique from the Structural School of family therapy and modified it for my use in working with CD families. Two of the major dimensions represented in this mapping technique are the nature of the relationships between members (represented by different lines between them) and a member's *apparent* power or influence (a larger figure has more apparent power than a smaller one).

The Map Legend explains the symbols:

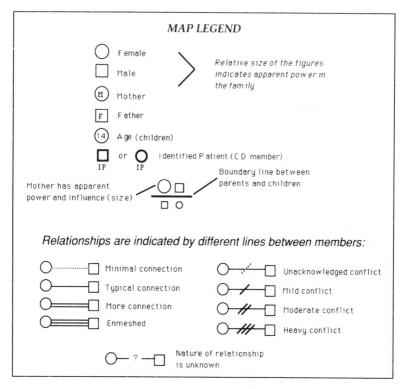

Below is a hypothetical map of a CD family in which the father is alcoholic:

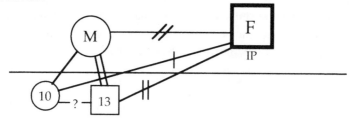

Figure 3.1. Family Map with Alcoholic Father

Figure 3.1 shows a typical map that could be drawn by the therapist after an initial session with a CD family. The father (IP)—emotionally distant but powerful—is in open and moderate conflict with mother and 13-year-old son. Mother is protective of the children, especially the son. The son is also close to and protective of the mother, which contributes to the conflict between him and his father, especially during active periods of alcohol use in the family. The daughter is the "lost child" who tries to stay clear of the mother-father-son turmoil. The nature of the relationship between the daughter and son is unknown after the initial interview.

The map in Figure 3.1, drawn from the therapist's impressions in the first interview, generates several observations and questions to be explored in future sessions:

1. The son's siding with the mother could put him in danger with the father, especially during the father's alcohol-use periods. Do we need to consider physical safety issues in this family?
2. It is likely that the mother is the "peacemaker" between father and son. If so, does this put her under extreme stress?
3. The daughter may be in a stressful triangle with mother and father—if she sides with one, she betrays the other.
4. Does the father have an ally outside the immediate family (parent, sibling, friend, etc.)? If so, will this person be a positive or negative influence on his recovery from chemical dependence?

For the family to begin adjusting its relationships for stable recovery, the father may need to assume a different parenting role once he becomes serious about abstinence from alcohol. Will he and the mother cooperate in his having a different, perhaps more active, parenting role? Does he want to begin rebuilding his relationship with his children, especially his son?

Obviously, families do not come to the first session carrying their organizational chart. In fact, most families don't think of the family in terms of structure. To construct a map, the therapist must piece together information through observations: who sits next to whom; who speaks to whom most often; who avoids eye contact with whom; who does the most and least talking; who gives and receives anger; who comforts a person when he or she cries or becomes upset. Did the husband show nonverbal disagreement by rolling his eyes when the wife was talking about the daughter? What did the mother do when the father became angry at the son?

These and similar observations will allow the therapist to piece together a tentative picture of the family structure. No single piece of information is meaningful, but taken together, all these behaviors create a general impression that can be diagrammed.

Clinical Uses for Maps

A map is useful in several ways. First, it organizes the therapist's perceptions of a family. Just the act of drawing relationships between the members helps the therapist sort out thoughts and feelings about the family as a unit, allowing him or her to make impressions and assumptions explicit and visible. The therapist needs to remain aware of his or her impressions of the family structure. Consciously or unconsciously, these assumptions and impressions direct and organize the therapy.

Second, a map is a way of sharing with colleagues the therapist's ideas. When discussing a family, it is useful to draw a picture, something the colleagues and therapist can see, point to, and talk about, without having to rely entirely on a verbal description. A map also serves as a visual aid for basic family data—age, sex, role relationships, and number of people.

Third, mapping reveals unanswered questions about relationships in the family; it points out gaps in the therapist's knowledge. Drawing lines between members can focus the therapist's attention on what he or she doesn't yet know about the nature of a relationship (as between the siblings in Figure 3.1). The missing information can be obtained in the next interview.

Fourth, maps help maintain a systems focus. Therapists won't become preoccupied with an individual or with only one relationship if the map presents a more global picture. The map is also a reminder to include others outside the home who may be important influences ("The family talked a lot about Uncle Joe—he belongs on the map; the school counselor has been seeing the child—put her on the map."). Finally, a map can indicate a broad direction for therapy. The therapist can look at it and spot major power imbalances, splits, and alliances in the family structure. For example, Figure 3.2 is another map. What's wrong in this picture?

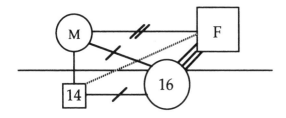

Figure 3.2. Map of a Hypothetical Family

The figures show a large difference in size (apparent power) between parents; the older child is larger than the mother and placed above the parent/child boundary, indicating power and influence out of proportion to the daughter's appropriate role in the family. The father and daughter are overinvolved (enmeshed), and the daughter is in open conflict with her mother and brother. The son-father bond is weak. If the mother appeared that small (passive) to the therapist, the daughter that large and powerful, and the father and daughter so close, it may be wise to explore these observations in the next session.

If the family in Figure 3.2 were a CD family, who would most likely be the identified patient? The daughter is a candidate. She could be using chemicals, enabled by the father and by the conflict between the parents, both of whom would be unable to unite and present clear, consistent limits to their daughter. Another possibility is the mother.

Her alcohol or other drug use could be isolating her from the family and creating conflicts and distance between her and the others.

In some family maps that resemble the one in Figure 3.2, the mother has been the IP or CD member, and in others, the adolescent who is overinvolved with one parent (the daughter in Figure 3.2) has been the IP. With severe power imbalances and splits in the family, the CD member could be one of several, and sometimes more than one.

Characteristics of Maps

A therapist's map may remain constant over several sessions with a family, or it may change over time. A map drawn after the first interview, then drawn again after the third interview, may show a different picture. As we learn more about the family relationships, our perceptions often change.

How accurate are these pictures? When different therapists view a family session through a one-way mirror and map the family afterwards, generally their pictures are quite similar, even though they did not discuss the family before drawing. There are always differences in their maps, of course, but usually only in the finer points.

A map is a useful clinical tool for understanding a family, but therapists must guard against elevating it to the status of a fact. It is only the opinion of one person about complex relationships among other people. A map is the therapist's current working hypothesis and is subject to change as new information is gathered. As with all clinical impressions, therapists must stand ready to change their minds.

One variation on the basic map is the "ecomap," a broader picture of the entire network, including extended family, friends, school or church contacts, boyfriends or girlfriends, deceased family members, other helping professionals involved with the family members, or other sources of influence within or outside the family. Also, therapists can put themselves on the map. This can be enlightening. With whom has the therapist joined? From whom does the therapist feel distanced?

Therapists can experiment with the mapping technique as a clinical tool and adapt it for their own purposes. Its value is twofold: (1) to visually display impressions and assumptions so that they can be examined, and (2) to help therapists think systemically about relationships and possible directions for change. When trying to make sense of a family structure, a picture is worth at least a thousand words.

Case Example

The Shaw family—father (Frank), mother (Sue), son (Stan, age 19) and daughter (Beth, age 13)—came to therapy because the parents were worried about the son's drinking. The father made the appointment. The map in Figure 3.3 was drawn after the initial interview.

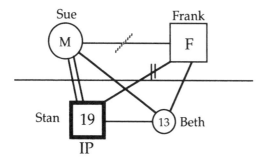

Figure 3.3. Case Example (Shaw Family)

Frank, the nominal head of the family, was in open conflict with Stan. Sue and Stan were emotionally closer, leading to her unintentional enabling of his drinking and a coalition between them. During the first interview, no disagreements or conflicts between the parents were acknowledged. Beth was not a problem for the parents and played the silent "good child" in the family. Stan, who held a part-time job, would consume the equivalent of a fifth or more of liquor daily for several consecutive days, but he defended his drinking as being under control and not interfering with his own or with his family's life.

During the initial interview Frank did most of the talking. Sue politely deferred to him, adding to or slightly modifying his story rather than having one of her own. Stan was restless and defensive during the session and angry toward his father. The mother softened the mutual accusations of Frank and Stan, and generally found ways to excuse the son's behavior, even though she was obviously worried about his drinking and his safety. The Shaws said there was no involvement by extended family or anyone outside the home.

Stan refused treatment for his alcohol problem. This made the initial goal for the therapy clear: help the parents use their united influence to get Stan into inpatient treatment. I referred the parents to Al-Anon and to the Family Orientation Program at the treatment center where I worked. During subsequent family sessions, I encouraged the parents to come together and agree about how to react to their son's alcoholic behavior. I hoped they would refuse to allow Stan's alcohol use while he lived at home. If they were able to do this, I suspected that the son would violate these limits during the few weeks the family would come for therapy sessions. The sessions would help the parents be prepared for this outcome.

By the third interview, I changed the map slightly:

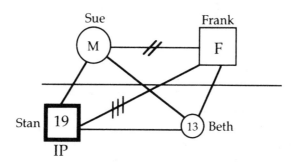

Figure 3.4. Case Example (Shaw Family), Third Session

The conflict between the parents became more open, and the father-son conflict was more intense. To help the parents work out their agreements with each other, I saw them separately without their children. My purpose was to encourage Frank and Sue to stand together and use their united influence to get Stan into inpatient treatment. After two more sessions with the parents, they were able to say to their son: "If you continue to drink and refuse inpatient treatment, you cannot live with us." They gave this ultimatum to Stan after the fifth session. He went into an inpatient treatment program for six weeks, and soon after discharge, he enlisted in the army.

By the sixth and final session I saw the family like this:

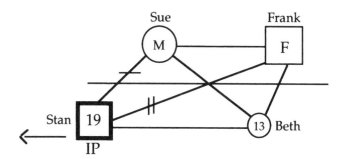

Figure 3.5. Case Example (Shaw Family), Final Session

Frank and Sue's disagreements and conflicts about how to react to Stan's drinking had been lessened, resulting in the mother and father becoming closer and more united. This caused more distance between Sue and Stan, thus diminishing Stan's power in the family. The father-son relationship was still distant and conflictual, and Beth remained a "good child." I encouraged Frank and Sue to continue the family sessions, but they were satisfied with the outcome and decided to stop.

Eighteen months later Frank called me and reported that Stan was doing well in the army but was struggling to keep his drinking from getting him in trouble. Frank also requested a session with himself and his wife to talk about Beth's secretive behavior, her poor school work, and her unfortunate choice of friends. The parents suspected that she was experimenting with drugs. We had two more sessions, repeating much of the initial work of Sue and Frank "speaking with one voice" to their daughter. The parents, more united this time, confronted Beth about her use. During follow-up a year later, the parents reported that Beth had "straightened out" and was doing well at home and in school.

In the Shaw case, mapping kept me aware of my ideas of how the patterns in the family—especially the mother-father conflict and the mother-son alliance—contributed to maintaining and enabling the son's alcohol problem. I shared this map with my colleagues, whose comments refined my picture and helped me decide on a therapeutic direction to take for this family's recovery. Mapping kept the forest in view while I was maneuvering among the trees.

The "Ideal" Family

Mapping assumes that we have an ideal picture in our heads about what a family should look like; otherwise, we could not discriminate between healthy and unhealthy family maps. Our values become apparent when we talk about the mother being much smaller on the map than the father, a child being larger than a parent, a parent and child's figures overlapping. When we say the map looks "wrong," we must have a "right" to compare it to, a standard about how families should look on paper. Again, it is important to make our values and assumptions explicit. Figure 3.6 is a map of an "ideal" family.

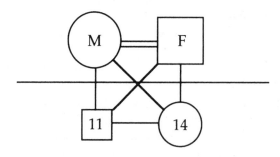

Figure 3.6. An "Ideal" Family

Figure 3.6 shows the following:
1. The mother-father bond is the strongest in the family.
2. Mother and father are of equal size.
3. Children are below the parent-child boundary.
4. The children are smaller than the parents.
5. The older child is slightly larger than the younger.
6. The map has no conflict lines.

Obviously, not many families look like that, certainly not all the time. Figure 3.6 is an ideal or model, a standard by which to measure positive or negative change. It is a goal toward which our therapy with chemically dependent families should aim.

What is "Normal"? When?

A functional or dysfunctional family map will look different at different developmental stages of the family. For example, Figure 3.7 portrays a map of a family that is appropriate and functional when the children are young.

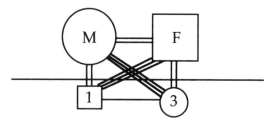

Figure 3.7. A "Normal" Family

This much family closeness may be appropriate and healthy when the children are young, but it would not be healthy as the children mature and prepare to leave home. Fifteen years later, the same family (Figure 3.8) with the same degree of closeness would be considered an enmeshed system. The members are so emotionally fused and connected that maturation and separation of the children from the parents would be difficult.

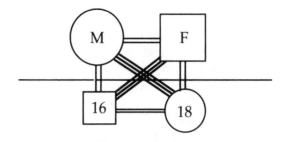

Figure 3.8. An Enmeshed Family

What constitutes "normal" or "functional" in family relation-ships? There are many ways to be a successful family, and if a family is working well therapists should leave it alone. However, CD families with symptomatic members come to the attention of therapists because something is no longer working. When a CD family comes for treatment, the therapist needs some basic assumptions about what is wrong and what might work better. Although therapists may have different ideas of what is healthy and unhealthy in family relationships, most therapists agree on certain fundamentals about family functioning. Here are some values and clinical assumptions to consider:

1. The mother-father relationship is primary. It existed before the children came and will exist after they leave. The parents are the responsible adults in the home, and their decisions will have the most effect on the family system. Also, the nature of the mother-father bond has more repercussions on the family than any other relationship; conflict between parents generally affects everyone in a family to a greater extent than conflict between any other two members. Conversely, a close parental bond is critical to the family's surviving all the inevitable crises and changes through which families must pass.

2. Parents should be in charge of and responsible for their children, more so when the children are young and less so as they mature. A family is not a democracy. Everyone doesn't have an equal

vote unless the parents agree to give the children equal influence on a particular family decision.

3. Parents own the home and should be responsible for what
   happens in it. If one child's alcohol or other drug use is causing
   trouble and chaos for everyone, parents have the obligation to
   intervene for the child's health and safety and to keep the home
   a decent place to live for themselves and for their other children.

4. A cross-generational coalition—one parent and one or more
   children sided against the other parent—spells trouble. If a
   father remains extremely close to his son, for example, favoring
   him over the other children, this alliance can create conflict
   between mother and father when father joins the son against her
   during tough periods in the child's development. Also, the son
   will likely have conflicts with his mother and siblings, who may
   be jealous or resentful of his close relationship with father. If
   the son is a CD adolescent, we have double trouble. Protection
   and enabling by the father is likely. This allows the son to gain
   power over the mother while progressing further in his illness.
   The family is likely to be emotionally split down the middle,
   with father-son on one side and mother-siblings on the other.

~~~~~~

Maps are tools to help the therapist maintain a systems orientation
to family therapy for chemical dependence. They make it easier for the
therapist to answer a central and important question: "How does this
family need to readjust its relationships in ways that make successful
recovery more likely for the entire family?" The answer to this
question has a direct influence on the therapist's goals in the early
stages of a family's recovery.

Family mapping can be used to determine which issues and
questions to explore in the family. Such exploration in a therapy
session teaches the therapist more about the family, thereby modifying
the family map. This, in turn, generates more questions and issues to

pursue. The process is circular and repetitive throughout therapy: obtain information from an interview; create a guess or hunch; explore the hunch; correct the information; create a new guess or hunch, etc. This self-correcting process, aided by maps, allows therapists to test the flexibility of the family and to discover its ability and willingness to change the relationship patterns which work against family recovery.

Of course, families are not objects on a blackboard, and shifting around their circles and blocks doesn't make them different. But this "organizational chart" approach does serve the valuable purpose of keeping the therapy focused on the family system, rather than on the individuals. Likewise, it helps the therapist achieve a systemic goal for the family's recovery. Once a therapist becomes thoroughly accustomed to the systems approach, mapping becomes less useful as a therapeutic tool.

Maps may be shown to families, and they usually find them interesting. But when doing this, the therapist should have a particular purpose in mind. For example, if the therapist wants to emphasize how peripheral and detached the IP was before his or her sobriety and how this is changing now that he or she is sober, the therapist can show the family the before-and-after maps. For such benevolent purposes, sharing a map with a family is productive. It isn't productive, however, to try to convince a family of unacknowledged enabling, side-taking, or over-involvement between members by pointing to a "factual" picture, which, in fact, has been drawn subjectively.

A family map is simply a clinical tool that helps therapists to be clear about the destination in therapy. Frequently, when the therapy gets lost, it's because therapists have forgotten where it's supposed to be going.

Common Patterns in CD Families

One of the main premises of this book—that interpersonal patterns in a CD family require treatment for the long-term recovery of the whole family—culminates in this section, which maps, describes, and suggests therapeutic strategies for ten common patterns in CD families. These patterns are certainly not the only possible ones, but they are the ones I've encountered most frequently in conducting and supervising CD family therapy in a variety of inpatient and outpatient settings.

Chemically dependent families develop relationships which crystallize over time. Rather than flow with the normal developmental stages of family life, CD families tend to remain stuck in a survival mode. This survival mode may serve to keep the family intact, but the resulting emotional isolation, anger, and distancing are harmful to the growth of its members. Some patterns, such as buried and hardened conflicts, entrenched enabling, or severe co-dependence, can also contribute to maintaining the CD problem.

Keeping general patterns in mind provides the therapist with the flexibility and the wide-angle view of the systems approach to therapy. In the Good Child/Bad Child (Pattern 4), for example, the therapist should always keep the good child in the total picture. The therapist needs to recognize what kind of pressure this child is under and how the parental relationship with the good child contributes to making the bad child bad. In the Enmeshed Child IP Pattern (Pattern 3), the systems approach suggests therapeutic alternatives to prying the parent and child apart. Other family relationships are used to influence the overinvolved parent and child, creating a more appropriate distance between the enmeshed pair.

As most family therapists have learned, patterns in families are not that difficult to identify. Interactions between members are repetitive; a family operates within a relatively narrow range of unspoken rules and unseen boundaries, which define its internal relationships. But about the time therapists believe they have a family figured out, the family will do something unexpected. In CD families, unpredictability is predictable, crises are frequent, and physical and emotional danger is a reality.

Before going into these common CD patterns, there are some qualifications to be made. Several important variables are crucial to the therapist's interventions but cannot be indicated in a family map. These variables include:

1. The severity of the alcohol or other drug use by the identified patient (IP) and the strength of his or her desire to recover.
2. The personalities of the family members, the amount of family denial and resistance, and the strength of the members' desire to preserve the family.
3. Race, cultural, and community attitudes and values, especially around the use of legal or illegal drugs, including alcohol.
4. Special conditions such as physical or mental handicaps of one or more family members.
5. Extended family influence, especially the influences of the parents' families of origin.

What follows are not cookie-cutter prescriptions; families are too complex for that. Rather, what follows is a *way to think* about family patterns and about how to change them. For example, three generational maps or maps depicting complicated extended families are not included in the common patterns, even though two or three generations of chemically dependent members are common, and a family system in treatment often includes extended members such as grandparents, in-laws, aunts or uncles. This omission is made for reasons of simplicity. Picturing and describing these more complex family systems would, in my judgment, be too complicated and laborious an introduction to systems therapy for CD problems. My goal is to convey the basic principles of the systems approach. I leave it to the therapist to discern the systemic way of thinking from the simple examples and to apply the principles to more complicated three generational and extended family situations.

60

All the cases that follow in this chapter, and throughout the book, assume that the IP is in treatment and that the family is attending conjoint sessions as part of the treatment program. Accordingly, each map represents a family in early recovery.

The maps show CD family *types*. Naturally, this or that particular family will only approximate the examples or types. Rather than a pure form, the therapist is likely to find degrees of similarity with any of these structures. To simplify the explanation of working with patterns, I have given each family two children, a son and daughter. To make the patterns more universal, I have omitted the ages of the children, even though this is usually specified on maps. If the IP is a child, his or her age is assumed to be in the teens or early adulthood. Both children are living with the parents.

Regarding gender, each pattern reflects my most common clinical experience with families. The majority of single-parent families I have treated, for example, have been parented by mothers, and the majority of stepparents have been male. Obviously, however, chemical dependents and co-dependents come in both sexes, and the suggested interventions apply when the gender is reversed in the mapped pattern.

Below each map, the *Pattern Description* describes some of the relationship issues and likely emotional climate of the mapped family. Its purpose is to introduce some of the composite characteristics of the pattern.

The *General Therapeutic Direction* for each map gives a brief statement of the desirable changes in the relationship patterns regarding closeness, distance, and conflict. This is the therapist's roadmap or therapeutic theme that guides the general direction of the therapy. In a given case, other directions are possible. Generally, therapeutic directions should be stated in broad terms and as simply as possible. They can usually be discovered by the question, "Besides maintaining sobriety, what am I trying to help this family accomplish in terms of its relationship patterns?"

The *Suggested Strategies* section lists possible interventions. Unless otherwise stated, each suggested intervention is made while everyone is in the session. Thus, the strategy will specifically mention if, for example, the children should not be present for the intervention.

As a preview, the ten patterns are listed below. The first five describe traditional, natural-parent families, and the second five are blended, single-parent, and divorced families. It is important to note that any of the five traditional patterns could be considered blended families for the purposes of the *General Therapeutic Direction* and *Suggested Strategies* if the special characteristics discussed for blended families are taken into account. The legend for the map symbols may be found at the beginning of this chapter on page 46.

Pattern #	Name
1	Peripheral Parent IP
2	Parent in the Middle
3	Enmeshed Child IP
4	Good Child / Bad Child
5	Triangulated Child IP
6	Blended Family - Child IP
7	Blended Family - Stepparent IP
8	Single Parent - Child IP
9	Single Parent IP
10	Divorced - Child IP

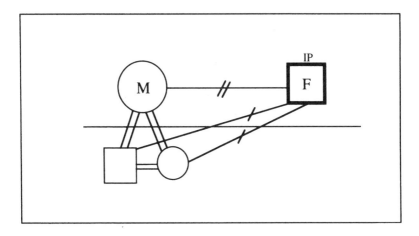

Pattern #1
Peripheral Parent IP

Pattern Description

This is perhaps the most common pattern in CD families when a parent is the identified patient (IP). The non-CD spouse and children have formed an emotional alliance for survival, leaving the IP on the fringe of being both a spouse and a parent. The survival structure is in place: "us against him." The parents are in open conflict; this affects the children more negatively than many parents realize.

The older the children, the greater the potential for conflict between them and the IP father, especially if a teenage son is trying to be the protective "man of the house." The mother's primary concerns are the arguments in the family and the protection of the children from the effects of the IP's chemical use. Her stress level is likely to be the highest in the family.

General Therapeutic Direction

To help the family accommodate to the reentry of the recovering father into a role-appropriate place in the family.

Suggested Strategies

1. A new relationship needs to develop between the father and his children. To accomplish this, the therapist must manage the mother's influence carefully. She is not likely to trust the father in a new parenting role and may sabotage any changes between father and children. The therapist must get the mother's cooperation during any interventions in the father-children relationships.
2. Encourage mother and father to make joint decisions about parenting.
3. Pay close attention to the mother:
   a. She is overly responsible and has carried a heavy load for a long time. When the father stays free of chemicals for a few weeks and becomes stronger, she may allow herself to show more weakness.
   b. Resentment by the mother is usually centered around her anger at the father for abandoning her and the children: "You were never here for the kids. You can't just march back in and take over as if nothing happened."
   c. The mother needs close support and help. Al-Anon referral is especially important, plus any other support group available.
4. Focus on the children:
   a. This gets the father's attention, since he probably feels some guilt toward them.
   b. During sobriety the father may begin to look at his children differently; he realizes that he doesn't really know them, especially if one or more are adolescents.
   c. Mother can help reintroduce father to the children. Their talk about the children brings them closer together as parents.
   d. Some recovering fathers see their children as acting poorly, as "bad kids." The therapist should try to Reframe (see Chapter 5) his view to children who are "upset," "scared," or "confused." This can soften the father's reaction to them.
5. Explore the father's support system. Besides his treatment and recovery program, who are his allies (friends, parents, siblings, etc.)? Who is he likely to go to for emotional support during early

recovery? The father's continued sobriety is the highest priority in therapy.

6. Discuss and normalize the family's lack of trust of father's sobriety (see Chapter 9).

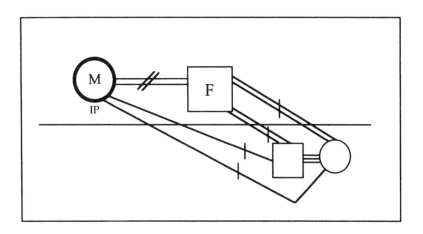

Pattern #2
Parent in the Middle

Pattern Description

Whereas Pattern #1 (Peripheral Parent IP) is a "two camp" family—a parent and children in one camp and the peripheral parent in the other—in this pattern the parent in the middle has one foot in both camps.

In the map, the father is in the middle between mother and children. He is not sided with the children against mother, but because of the mother's chemical dependence, neither can he join with her to provide consistent parenting; he is caught in the go-between role of peace keeper. Protecting the children is a top priority for him, but so is preserving the family. The middle parent is in a highly stressful position; he is a super-caretaker and gallantly tries to be all things to all family members.

The children add to the stress by becoming angry at both parents: at the CD parent because of her use, and at the non-CD parent for not being able to stop her from using or, in extreme cases, for not leaving her. The children form a coalition with each other for their mutual protection. In severe cases, the older child may even act as the protective guardian for the younger. The family stress, however, is likely to cause conflicts between them.

General Therapeutic Direction

To move the parents toward a parental alliance for the children.

Suggested Strategies

1. Explore the parents' willingness for the mother to spend more time with the children without the father. Because of lack of trust and other factors, this should go slowly at first. Be aware that the father may be reluctant to give up his illusion of control in the family.
2. Keep the father central and influential in all change interventions. He has been the hub of the family wheel for a long time and is likely to stay that way until trust in the recovering mother is reestablished. He usually has the power and influence either to support or to sabotage any change.
3. To avoid adding stress, which may contribute to the IP's relapse, she should be given only those new family responsibilities she is willing to accept.
4. Explore the mother-father relationship, especially around parenting. Do not get into their spousal relationship (intimacy, sex, in-law issues, etc.) too quickly.
5. Watch for the father trying to become the mother's treatment "sponsor," pushing her to attend meetings or counseling her about sobriety. The father should be explicitly encouraged to let his wife be responsible for her own recovery.
6. Explore the father's stress. Ask about his list of physical stress symptoms. This increases the mother's and the children's attention

toward him and lays the groundwork for him to attend his own recovery program.

7. Explore the emotional life of the children by having separate interviews with them if necessary. Drawings (see Chapter 5) are useful for this purpose. Explain to the parents that the children's feelings of anger and fear are normal, but that once the family is stable, their emotions may surface in an unexpected way such as becoming moody for no apparent reason, emotionally withdrawing, overreacting to mild frustration, and the like.

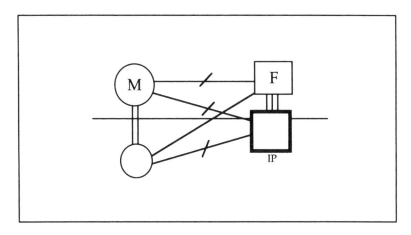

Pattern #3
Enmeshed Child IP

Pattern Description

The adolescent IP has always been the father's favorite child. The father has unintentionally enabled his son's chemical use by being permissive toward him and by denying the extent of his CD problem. Because of the father's influence, the mother has difficulty setting appropriate limits on the son. By standing with his father, the son sometimes has more power than his mother. The parents often disagree more than they admit to; their conflicts begin to surface once they are urged to unite to present clear limits to their son's CD behavior.

The father and daughter have an unconflicted relationship, but the daughter is fully aware that her brother can usually get his way with the father. She is emotionally closer to the mother and may have frequent conflicts with her brother.

General Therapeutic Direction

To decrease the son's power by reducing the father-son overinvolvement. The less inappropriate power the parents give to the son, the less likely enabling will continue.

Suggested Strategies

1. Add distance between father and son by bringing mother and father closer together. To the degree this happens, the father-son overinvolvement will be reduced.
2. During the sessions, clearly support the mother and father as heads of the family, while treating the son as an adolescent who must live by the parents' rules. Because of the son's power in the family, this should be done carefully; he may have enough influence to stop the family sessions.
3. Three ways to make the father-son distance more appropriate are:
   a. Bring mother and father together around their concern for son's recovery.
   b. Using enactments (see Chapter 4), pair the father-daughter and mother-son in separate conversations. This unbalances the two camps by "crisscrossing" each parent with the more distant child.
   c. Work on the mother-son relationship. If it improves, father and son will become less enmeshed. This may also interrupt the father's enabling and give the mother, the stricter parent, more influence with the son.
4. Be alert for the father becoming the son's treatment "sponsor" (see

Chapter 9). The responsibility for recovery should be kept squarely on the son.

5. Meetings with the two parents together without the children are usually necessary. Their purpose is to help the parents negotiate their agreements regarding how they should respond as a parental team. What will they do together to present a clear and consistent direction for the son's recovery? What will they do if the son ignores their limits? What is their relapse plan (see Chapter 9)? What will happen if one parent stays firm on the agreements and the other weakens? How can they convince the son that they are serious about changes? When these issues are explored, the therapist is working on the parents' relationship while keeping the child's CD problem as the focus.

6. Spread the parental concern to the non-IP child, in the mapped example, the daughter. Explain the "stair-stepping" phenomenon to parents, namely, that sometimes, when the older child becomes drugfree, another adolescent steps up to take his or her place in the glamorous and daring world of alcohol or other drug use. To avoid this, the daughter needs to see the strict limits imposed by the parents on the son; she is then less likely to follow in his footsteps. Focusing on the daughter takes some of the heat and pressure off the son. It can also increase the parents' motivation to work out their parenting relationship toward the IP child. Going through this family crisis again with another child is a horrifying idea to most parents.

7. In limit-setting talk from parents to son, encourage the father to take the lead. This strict talk from the more lenient parent shows the son that something different is happening in the family.

8. Explore the sibling relationship by encouraging the siblings to talk with each other on a relevant topic. Resentment may be high between them. The daughter resents the favoritism the son receives from the father and the family embarrassment and conflict caused by her brother's chemical use. The son resents his "good kid" sister, whom he knows is no angel but who manages to stay out of trouble.

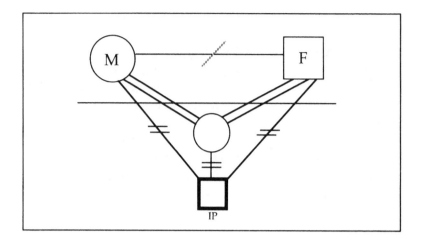

Pattern #4
Good Child / Bad Child

Pattern Description

The CD adolescent is the bad child, the scapegoated member of the family. The other child is the good child, the "perfect" daughter. The bad child is often uncooperative at home and causes trouble and family embarrassment with legal and school problems. He is usually closer to his peer group than to the family, and the parents are exasperated over what to do with him. In stark contrast, the good child excels socially, at home, and at school. She is usually close to the parents, rarely upsets them, and is an enduring source of parental pride.

The good child is as much above the norm as the bad child is below. A balance is maintained—the good child excels to the degree the bad child fails. Sibling conflict is intense, partly maintained by the parental favoritism.

The relationship between the parents appears benign, or even close. Typically, the parents do not acknowledge major disagreements or conflict between them, at least not at first. On the surface, the only problems in this family are caused by the IP, with family arguments centering around the bad child, often locking into a three-against-one coalition. This side-taking is acutely felt by the CD adolescent, although it's not usually acknowledged by the other members.

The adolescent is usually uncooperative in treatment. He is a frustrated, angry young man, and removing the chemicals does little to diminish his hostile moods.

General Therapeutic Direction

To help family members bring to the surface and resolve the underlying tension and conflict that they are avoiding by maintaining the IP as a scapegoat.

Suggested Strategies

1. In general, it's not a good idea for the therapist to try to protect a scapegoated member of a family, especially if it is a child. If the therapist sides with the child, it often redoubles the family's attack on him or her. This is the family's way of maintaining the scapegoat role to avoid looking at other problems in the family.
2. Work closely with the parents to help them make decisions about how to respond to the son. During this, be especially sensitive to the disagreements, hidden conflict, and tension between the parents.
3. When the son enters treatment and becomes drug free, encourage the parents to give him some privacy and breathing room. This is necessary because of the son's extreme anger at the family.
4. Prepare the parents for the son's anger after he stops using chemicals, even if he denies being angry.
5. Since the son feels that the rest of the family has ganged up on him, find out who his allies are: an extended family member, a friend, or another adult outside the home. These advocates for the son could be discussed, and if appropriate, invited to a session. The group or individual treatment counselor for the adolescent could also serve this purpose by attending one or more family sessions.

6. Sensitize the parents against making comparison statements about the two children. Explain that, even though the son brought this on himself by his behavior, statements by the parents comparing the brother with his sister are often more painful than he will admit. Ask the parents to remind each other not to use such statements if one of them should forget.

7. About the third session, begin to spread the concern to the good child, especially if she is younger than the IP. This distributes some of the focus, and helps the IP feel that the whole family, not just himself, is being looked at. To accomplish this, the following steps usually work.

   a. First, lay the groundwork by talking with and about the good child. Make the point that trying to be perfect is hard work.

   b. Say to the good child, "Somehow you've learned how to get what you want and still avoid your parents' anger."

   c. Explain to the parents that the pressure of being good and pleasing the parents adds more stress to their daughter than they probably realize. It would be well to watch her for signs of stress. It's even possible that she may one day experiment with alcohol or other drugs in her peer group.

      This talk about the good child undermines the aura of perfection surrounding her and dilutes the stark contrast between the children. It also alerts the parents to the burden being carried by both children.

8. Initially, let brother and sister monitor their own distance from each other, unless it seems possible to help them become closer or in some way improve their relationship.

9. Anticipate open or implied blackmail by the bad child: "If you don't let me have my way, you're causing me to return to using" (see Chapter 9). Parents will need each other's support to avoid this trap.

10. After several sessions, gently shift the focus to the parents to see if they will explore their relationship as *spouses*, possibly revealing some of the buried anger and tension between them that has been transferred to the scapegoated child. The children should not be present for this talk. A good introduction for this shift is, "A

problem like the one your son has can cause a lot of stress on a marriage. How has it affected yours?"

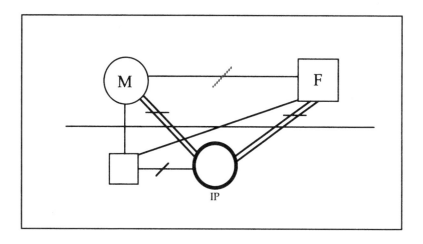

Pattern #5
Triangulated Child IP

Pattern Description

Parents who have deep-seated conflicts often detour, or triangulate, their conflicts through the IP child; the child becomes the medium through which they act out their disagreements or frustrations with each other. As parents, they are somewhat detached from each other and often do not acknowledge their conflicts. They seem to be parenting separately and are not in close communication about the IP child's activities. This pattern is common when both parents have busy careers.

The triangulated child finds this divided parenting a mixed blessing. On the one hand, she has more freedom since neither parent is sure how or with whom she spends much of her time. This freedom and autonomy draw her closer to her peer group and away from the family. On the other hand, the daughter is frequently caught between the parents, listening separately to different and often contradictory viewpoints. The parents may even put the daughter squarely in the middle by one parent countermanding the supervision of the other. No matter which way the daughter moves, she betrays one parent. Her escape has been to avoid parental contact whenever possible and to move toward peers and chemical use. Because of her autonomy, the daughter's use has gone undetected for a long period, giving her time to become chemically dependent. During treatment, when her extensive chemical use is uncovered, the parents are often shocked.

The other children in the family usually stay close to home and frequently cause no major problems for the parents.

General Therapeutic Direction

To strengthen the parental partnership by helping the parents reach agreements concerning the IP child. The desire to help their child and family motivates the parents to look at their relationship in the therapy sessions, first as parents and later as spouses.

Suggested Strategies

1. Encourage the parents to respect the daughter's right to privacy while maintaining knowledge of her whereabouts and activities. The parents should not expect the daughter's instant closeness with the family when she begins to abstain from chemicals.
2. Encourage the parents to allow the daughter to have appropriate peer contact during her recovery, e.g., spending the night at the house of a friend the parents know or inviting a friend to stay

overnight at their house. Parents cannot completely isolate her from her peers. These privileges, of course, would depend on the daughter remaining drug free.

3. Explore the son's role in the family—perfect child or lost child? Inform the parents that frequently a younger child is waiting to take a turn at being a difficult, even chemical-using teenager, and that the parents' successful handling of the daughter will be a strong prevention message to their son. Protection for this younger sibling can motivate the parents to unite and take care of the daughter's problems.

4. During the session openly identify the more strict and more lenient parent. Most parents will agree which one is more strict or lenient than the other. If the parents don't make a distinction, ask the children; they will usually identify which is which. The strict parent will need to help the lenient one stand firm when they are tested by the daughter to see if they can present firm and consistent limits on her behavior.

5. Use a maneuver I call "bumping the kid." At about the third or fourth session, separate the parents from the children by asking the parents' permission for the children to wait outside for the remainder of the session. Before they leave the room, occupy the chair vacated by the IP, moving it to a convenient position to talk with the parents. The therapist literally "bumps" the child by taking his or her place in the triangle. This symbolic gesture tells the child, "I will help your parents with their issues; you don't need to sacrifice yourself by being their go-between." This could also be stated explicitly.

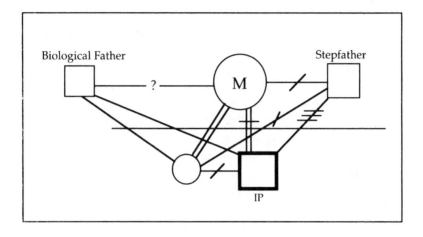

Pattern #6
Blended Family - Child IP

Pattern Description

In a blended family it is normal for the biological parent to be closer to his or her children than the stepparent; the older the children when the stepparent entered the family, the more this is true.

In the mapped example, the daughter is harmfully involved with alcohol and other drugs, and she and the stepfather are in heated conflict. The stepfather's direct anger at the daughter for disrupting the household—and his marriage—causes a natural protective reaction to emerge in the mother. This automatically puts mother and father in conflict. The older the daughter, the greater the clash between her and the stepfather, sometimes resulting in physical harm to someone in the family.

The mother is in an especially difficult spot. When she protects the daughter, she alienates her husband. She may also have frequent arguments with her daughter about her chemical use or about other disruptive or self-defeating behaviors.

By the time the family reaches treatment, the stepfather has long since figured out that his wife does not approve of some of his parenting with her children, especially in problem situations. When he tries to discipline his way, mother disapproves; she has never really given full permission for him to parent her children.

General Therapeutic Direction

To increase the cooperation between the parents around the child's recovery. Even though this is the same strategy with most two-parent households with a CD adolescent, in a blended family it's different. The therapist is well advised not to move toward a totally equal partnership in parenting as one might do in a natural parent family. Most blended families have a built-in imbalance, since it's natural for the biological parent to have more bonding with and more concern for the children than the stepparent.

Suggested Strategies

1. The first step is to find out the relationship of the blended family to the family of the biological father. If the biological father is involved, do the children have visitation privileges with him? What is the frequency of contact?
2. If the daughter regularly visits the biological father's household, a separate session with the biological parents and their children may be necessary. Both biological parents need to coordinate the rules of their respective houses, the supervision of the adolescent during recovery, the frequency of contact with the biological father, and other matters that affect the parenting of the teenager. The mother would be responsible to communicate with the stepfather the content of the session, and to get his consent to coparenting agreements made between the biological parents.
3. Most of the therapy, however, is with the household in which the teenager lives. Help the biological parent and stepparent reach some agreements on the "recovery rules" for the adolescent: curfew time, her responsibilities at home, peer group contact, a plan in case a

relapse occurs, and other important topics. Depending on the circumstances and the parents' desires, the children may or may not be present during this work.

4. The stepfather is usually angry, whether he admits it or not. He has little real authority with the IP child and tends to blame his wife for being too lenient with the children. To gain the stepfather's cooperation, the therapist needs to find ways to allow him to feel more in control, thereby decreasing his anger. This can be done in a variety of ways. Listen to the stepfather carefully. Strongly empathize with him (see *joining* in Chapter 4), regardless of how angry he is. Acknowledge his special and important position in the family and his desire to work through the difficulty and restore peace to the home. Ask his opinion frequently and keep him involved and active in the sessions. Acknowledge that to be helpful to himself and to his family as a parent, he must use his *own* style and personality. Of course, don't try to increase the stepfather's parenting control if his idea of discipline is physical or emotional abuse.

5. The main theme, given to the parents while the children are absent from the session, is contained in this question to the mother: "Under what conditions will you agree to your husband helping you with parenting your children?" Create an Enactment (see Chapter 4) around this question, getting the parents to talk to each other. If they get off the subject, gently bring them back to the question. It is important to make the conditions explicit and available for negotiation, even though the stepfather can reject the mother's conditions.

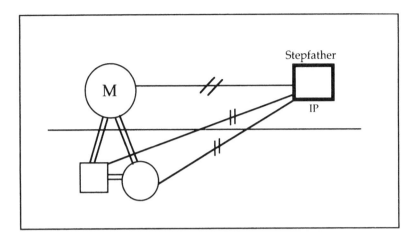

Pattern #7
Blended Family - Stepparent IP

Pattern Description

This pattern is similar to, but more extreme than, the Peripheral Parent IP (Pattern #1). In this pattern the stepfather is the "odd man out." A tight coalition of spouse and children has formed against him, and he is in open conflict with everyone.

The non-CD spouse, as usual, is in an intensely stressful situation. She must somehow manage her husband's disapproval of the children, protect the children from his influence while he's intoxicated, and react as a spouse to his alcohol or other drug problem. She is likely to be extremely protective of and close to her children, which the stepfather may deeply resent.

This pattern, like many in CD families, tends to be self-maintaining. Mother and children become closer when the stepfather shows anger at either of them; more parent-child closeness increases his anger, resulting in more closeness, etc. Mutual blaming between the parents also produces a stalemate:

Stepfather: "I drink because I'm shut out of the family."
Mother: "You're shut out of the family because you drink."

Tools and Techniques of the Family Systems Approach

General Therapeutic Direction

To define the stepfather's role in parenting the children. The mother-stepfather cooperation around parenting is more crucial than in a natural-parent family because of the strong conflict between the stepfather and one or more children.

Suggested Strategies

1. Find out about the extended family network. Do the children have contact with their biological father? Does the wife have contact with her ex-husband to arrange for child visitation, etc.? Is the visitation arrangement and contact with the biological father acceptable to the stepfather?
2. Because of the stepfather's alienated position in the family, identifying his allies is more important than in a traditional family. Whom does he go to when he needs to talk about what's happening in the family? Who is his support? How will he manage his feelings during sobriety? These and similar questions define his support system for recovery and recognize his difficult position in the family.
3. Be alert for signs of sexual abuse of a child, especially if the children are young. In this pattern several factors make it more likely than in other families: (1) the stepparent's alcohol or other drug use, (2) the emotional cutoffs and distance between the spouses, (3) the children's likelihood of being used in the power struggle between parents, (4) the non-blood relationship between stepparent and children.
4. Some other issues worth exploring:
   a. How can the mother help the stepfather feel more like an emotional part of the family?
   b. To what extent can the stepfather and children reestablish their relationship, at least partly independent of the mother? To what extent will the mother allow this?
   c. Can the mother give the stepfather total responsibility for his own recovery?

    d. How willing are the parents to explore intimacy, sex, emotional bonding, and other issues in the spousal relationship?

    e. Will the mother seek recovery groups for herself and her children?

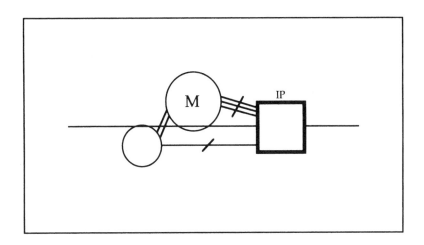

Pattern # 8
Single Parent - Child IP

Pattern Description

In this single parent family the mother and IP son are enmeshed. In the map, both mother and son cross the parent-child boundary: mother sometimes becomes more like a peer than a parent to the children, and sometimes the son acts more like a spouse or parent than a child. The son is the "man of the house" and takes the role seriously. Assuming he is the older child, the son has comforted mother through difficult times, including the divorce from his father. The daughter is also close to the mother but because she's usually younger and less of a support for the mother, the bond is not as tight as between the mother and the older child.

It is tempting to speculate that the son's alcohol or other drug problem is partly the result of his attempt to separate from the mother, to create an identity independent of her, and to escape the feelings of smothering closeness. These are feelings that he usually cannot or will not express directly. His communication is through rebellion, and alcohol or other drugs are a convenient choice.

The mother is likely to see her son's chemical use, peer group identification, and withdrawal from her as betrayal ("How could you do this to me?"). The son accuses her of overreacting and not understanding him. He does not enjoy hurting his mother—in fact, he is highly protective of her—but the drive toward peers and drugs is strong. Through all this, the mother and daughter may become closer.

In the past, the mother has probably offered inconsistent parenting to the children, vacillating between parent, friend, confidante, playmate, and partner-in-crisis. With the mother's incongruent roles—one day helpless and distraught, the next day an authoritarian parent—the children don't take her seriously as a parent, especially when she tries to set limits on their behavior.

These overinvolved parent-child situations are usually a two-sided affair—the mother holds tight to her son-partner-friend, while the son shows the normal ambivalence of adolescence by pushing his mother away with one hand and holding on to her with the other. By the time they reach treatment, the CD problem has caused considerable conflict, and the distance between them is greater than it's ever been.

General Therapeutic Direction

To help the parent find *adult* support for the many stresses experienced by single parents. Adult peer involvement decreases her need to use her relationship with her children for her emotional support and keeps her parental role more appropriate and consistent.

Suggested Strategies

1. Encourage adult support for the mother. This could come from professional sources such as the CD treatment center, other counseling, parent support groups, Al-Anon, Families Anonymous, or Parents Without Partners. Additional adult support could come from more immediate sources: extended family, co-workers, friends, or boyfriends.

2. If the mother is not dating, encourage her to think about it. Discuss how the children would react if she started dating, since a single parent frequently underestimates how far the children will go to discourage her. For reasons of jealousy, protectiveness, fear of loss, and resentment at someone taking their dad's place, the new man in the living room is not always welcomed by the children. If the mother decides to date, she should be prepared to get a reaction from the children and be prepared to stand firm on her decision.

3. Peer support is also needed for the CD son. Encourage the mother to allow the son to find new, non-using friends. Discuss her rules on the son's dating.

    [The above strategies are designed to interrupt the mother-son enmeshment by providing both of them *separate* sources of age-appropriate support and friendship. When the mother and son develop other important relationships, their strong emotional need for each other is reduced, allowing a healthier parent-child relationship.]

4. Explore the biological father's role, if any, in the family. Does he have contact with the children? Is he remarried? Do the children visit him where he lives? Do the divorced parents have agreements

about the children's behavior during their visits in the father's home? Is the mother fully aware of the son's level of supervision when at the father's house?

5. Explore the daughter's role in the family, her emotional state, and her desires and concerns. By the third or fourth interview, the daughter should be as actively involved in the sessions as the son. Is mother worried that the daughter may be the next to try alcohol or other drugs? Is she sure the daughter doesn't feel neglected, with all the attention going to the son's problem? Is the daughter trying so hard to be perfect that it causes her emotional difficulties the mother doesn't know about? Again, the strategy is to interrupt the mother-son overinvolvement by spreading the mother's attention more equally between the children.

6. Watch for the mother becoming the son's "sponsor" during his recovery, offering counseling, education about chemical dependence, AA or NA talk, or other treatment functions. If parents take this role, the recovering child always holds the ace card: when he gets angry at his mother, he relapses, showing her what a lousy counselor she is. To be valuable to her son, the mother needs to take better care of herself and leave the treatment to professionals. Make sure that she understands that her contribution is to maintain a caring, firm, and consistent stance toward her son's use of chemicals while he's living at home.

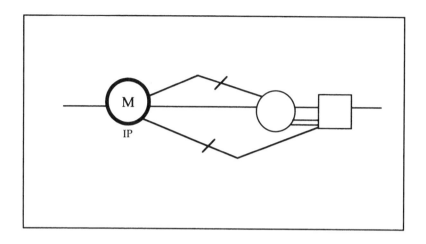

Pattern #9
Single Parent IP

Pattern Description

This is a "see-saw" family situation. The mother vacillates between being a parent, when she's sober and straight, and being a child, when she becomes incompetent through alcohol or other drug use. Conversely, the children must also alternate. During the mother's active chemical use, they are self-sufficient, sometimes becoming caretakers to the parent; during the mother's sober periods, they revert to being children.

Needless to say, this is a physically and emotionally dangerous situation for everyone, especially younger children. This family frequently comes to the attention of the state and/or local Department of Social Services (DSS) for child abuse or neglect.

Because of the undependable parenting and the severe role reversals, the children are forced to mature too fast. Although they can be quite independent and at times courageous, if the chemical dependence has been a problem for more than a year, the children should be

85

Tools and Techniques of the Family Systems Approach

expected to have moderate to severe emotional problems, even if they manage to avoid legal and school trouble and even if they appear on the surface to be unruffled. The grown-up mask hides a scared, angry child.

General Therapeutic Direction

To work closely with the mother and children to offer them support for the mother's recovery, both within her extended family or social network and in self-help recovery groups. The mother's *adult* support network is necessary to help her avoid burdening the children with her emotional issues during her early recovery.

Suggested Strategies

1. If necessary, use leverage from DSS or the courts during the mother's treatment. While in treatment, she should be gently and firmly given the choice of staying sober or having her children removed from the home. The safety needs of the family should be insured before family therapy is attempted.
2. Explore the mother's enabling system. Someone outside the immediate family is usually involved. It may be boyfriend(s), friends, parents, or extended family. If the mother has a boyfriend who uses alcohol or other drugs, her contact with him during her primary treatment or aftercare should be grounds for DSS to keep the case active for investigation.
3. If the mother becomes serious about recovery, she needs close support for an extended period. During and after treatment, a tight connection with AA, NA, or another self-help group will be necessary, plus any aftercare support groups available at the treatment center.
4. This family also needs other outside support: extended family, friends, professionals, DSS, or any source that can assist in child care while the mother works her recovery.

86

5. If the mother successfully abstains, support her competence and authority as a parent. This will probably be resisted by the children, especially if they are teenagers. There is too much anger and too little trust for them to suddenly accept her full authority as a parent.
6. Increase the mother's awareness of the children's normal anger in this situation, and how they may undermine her attempts to regain parental role. They may be accustomed to much freedom and won't take kindly to limit-setting. Make the prediction to the mother that the children will test her mightily to see if she's serious about taking charge.
7. Prepare the mother for the possibility that the children may unite against her. They have formed a close coalition for survival, and it may well continue until they are convinced the mother seriously intends to get well.
8. Convince the mother that her children need separate counseling and support and a chance to vent some of their pent-up anger and fear. At first, they may need to do this away from the mother.
9. Look for the "parentified child"—the older child who acted as substitute parent for the other children during the mother's incompetent periods. This child will be the key to the other children accepting or rejecting the mother's authority. Empathize with the parentified child (see *joining*, Chapter 4) and give him or her a full hearing in the therapy sessions. Normally, as the mother gets better, the therapist can expect a battle for control between the parentified child and the mother. For the sake of everyone, the mother must win this power struggle and regain her position as primary caretaker in the family.
10. Stay alert for possible chemical use in one or more children. During the mother's active chemical use, they may have started using alcohol or other drugs as their emotional escape from an unbearable situation; or they may start using as an expression of anger toward the parent.

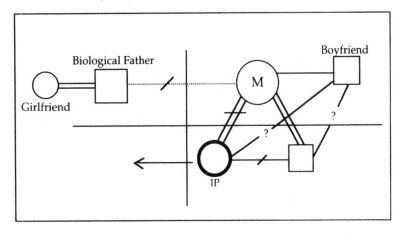

Pattern #10
Divorced - Child IP

Pattern Description

This pattern is presented with some assumptions: neither parent has remarried; each parent has a boyfriend or girlfriend; and the children have visitation privileges with the non-custodial parent who is also available for family sessions. If the biological father is not involved, this pattern has many of the characteristics and suggested strategies of Pattern #8, Single Parent - Child IP.

If the parents have a joint custody or visitation arrangement, this is a two-household situation for the recovering adolescent. She lives with the mother and has regular visits with the father, either overnight or for several days. For an adolescent trying to give up alcohol or other drugs, this arrangement can be precarious. If the parents don't communicate closely about the daughter, one household doesn't know what she does at the other. The daughter may even have two sets of peers, one in each location. If both parents are not invested in the daughter's recovery, she could continue her use while visiting one without being detected by the other. Also, the daughter probably lives under a different set of rules for each house. This can lessen the stability and consistency necessary for her recovery.

General Therapeutic Direction

To facilitate the divorced parents' cooperation with each other to help their daughter's recovery.

Suggested Strategies

1. The mother is the person most likely to have made the initial contact for the daughter's CD treatment. Invite everyone who lives in her home to the first interview, including the boyfriend, if he lives there.
2. During the first interview define the family system: the boyfriend's place in the situation; the frequency and number of visits of children with the father; the occupants of the father's house; involvement by grandparents or other extended family; and close family or non-family relationships. This information defines the potential enabling system for the recovering daughter. Also, with such a volatile mixture of parental influences, determine whether the children are caught in the angry cross fire of the adult relationships. If so, support the mother's responsibility and authority to manage these relationships by making the final decision about the daughter's activities (assuming the mother has primary legal custody).
3. If the IP's contact with the father is significant, explore with the mother the possibility of her attending a session with the father and their children; the boyfriend would not be included. The purpose is to encourage the parents to cooperate in helping their daughter stay drug free and to explore the effects of her recovery on the other children. The purpose is not to uncover and resolve old issues between the ex-spouses or to discuss their respective adult relationships and love life. The session is strictly limited to their cooperation in helping their daughter recover from her chemical dependence.

4. If the mother agrees to a joint session with the father and children, the session should help the parents communicate about the daughter's visitation schedule, her recovery program, the possibilities for relapse, the parents' plan if this occurs, how the other children are coping, and other issues that are important to them as parents.

5. Of particular concern are the amount and type of chemical use occurring in the home of the father. Does he use alcohol, prescription, or non-prescription drugs? Does his girlfriend? Are the father and mother familiar with the daughter's peer groups associated with both homes, and do they know whether the peers use alcohol or other drugs? Explain how difficult it is for teenagers to abstain if those around them are using.

6. If the mother is concerned about chemical use in the home of the father, encourage her to renegotiate her daughter's visitation schedule, through the court if necessary. She should be prepared to take whatever action is necessary to keep her child away from a substance-using environment.

7. If the relationship between the mother and boyfriend has lasted for a year or more, inquire about their intentions towards each other. Have they discussed a more permanent arrangement, like marriage? How do the children and boyfriend get along? Are the children clear on the mother-boyfriend relationship? Explain that you are asking these questions for the benefit of her children, who may be anxious, confused, and even hostile if they don't understand the relationship. The children may not form a close attachment with the boyfriend because they resent him for trying to take their father's place, or they're afraid the boyfriend may disappear if they start to get emotionally closer to him. Encourage the mother to be as clear with the children as she can about her intentions with a long-standing boyfriend relationship.

~~~~~~

The following summarizes the general principles of the systems approach with all CD families:

1. Include all children living in the home, whether the IP is a parent or a child. The welfare of children is often the strongest motivation for family recovery.

2. Always consider the broader context within which recovery will take place: extended family, friends, other professionals helpers. The more people involved in the therapy, or in the therapist's thinking about the case, the more influences are available for therapeutic change.

3. Emphasize separate self-help recovery groups for the family members. Some of the healing is done in the family, and some is best done away from the family members. This is also their long-term support for crises, adjustments to the family sobriety, and the other inevitable problems that will arise.

4. Pursue therapeutic goals, based on the structural characteristics of the family. This is not an "anything goes" type of therapy in which every session is a new beginning. Pursuing a definite direction based on the clinician's view of the family will provide more information and feedback than undirected pursuit of random issues.

5. When the IP is a child, try to bring parents together in an alliance with each other around the problem. Work on the parental relationship while keeping the presenting CD problem and person in focus. This approach has several rationales:

    a. The CD is primary; it is not a secondary or symptomatic problem, one that can be put aside until later. Primary and separate treatment for the CD member is the first priority.

b. How the parents—acting together—respond to the problem is an important factor in whether or not the young person abstains from alcohol or other drugs. Parental unity and consistency give the IP child a clear and convincing message about abstinence.

c. We can assume that the parents' relationship is under stress and needs help, partly as a result of the child's chemical problem. Supporting the parents, who have the most influence on the family functioning, is the best short- and long- term benefit for the family and for the CD child.

d. Improving the parental partnership is also prevention work, especially if younger siblings are in the home. If parents pull together and react successfully to the IP child, they may prevent a similar problem if a younger child later takes his or her turn at alcohol or other drug use or at other destructive behavior.

6. With a parent IP, primary emphasis should still be on the spouse/parent relationship. The rationales for this approach are:

a. The mother-father relationship has the greatest effect on how the recovering parent and the family fares during recovery.

b. The non-CD parent has been either highly stressed and needs help from his or her spouse or needs to explore his or her own issues of power, control, and co-dependence in relation to the CD spouse.

7. In a single parent or divorced household, support for the parent should be the primary focus. The improved functioning of this person, whether he or she is newly sober or has a recovering child, is crucial for the family recovery.

Chapter 4
Four Basic Techiniques

Most therapists learned a standard set of techniques to work with individuals: listening, empathizing, reflecting, clarifying, and interpreting. The model presented here provides four others to use in working with family dynamics: *joining* establishes rapport between the therapist and the family members; *assigning tasks* provides between-session assignments for the family; *creating enactments* encourages conversations between family members; and *segmenting* subdivides the family for a particular therapeutic purpose. These fundamental techniques access the powerful interactional aspect of therapy with families.

This chapter will explain each of these four essential techniques and how they apply to working with CD families. One or more of these fundamentals has rescued me from many a tight spot during family sessions.

Joining

Joining is the process a therapist uses to make a workable connection between himself or herself and the family members—establishing rapport and trust, communicating empathy, showing respect, being patient and supportive, and seeing the family's view of reality, individually and collectively. It is vital in most forms of therapy, but it's even more important with families because of the need to gain cooperation in spite of multiple, and often conflicting, viewpoints within the family.

The therapist joins the family by:

— actively listening
— supporting individual and family strengths
— accommodating the family's values and style
— using their words and metaphors
— matching their mood, at least initially
— communicating understanding
— expressing genuine concern
— benevolently challenging their restricted view of themselves and their situation
— giving them hope

Joining is to therapy as staying on key is to singing—it's a vital part of the activity, not a technique to be used only at certain times. The therapist is always doing it, to a greater or lesser degree. There's a saying among family therapists: "There's no such thing as resistant families, only those inadequately joined." That may be overstating the point, but not by much.

Most people who have an alcohol or other drug use problem are pressured into seeking treatment by the law, by an employer, by their family, or by their own pain and suffering. Treatment is usually a last resort. They've been backed into a corner and are understandably frustrated and angry when they walk in the door. Careful joining makes them less angry when they walk out. Most CD professionals know this and are adept at managing the CD client's anger at being forced into treatment.

The family's anger and resistance is also understandable. The family members have put up with and have been tortured by a family member's chemical use for months or years and now we request that they be a part of the treatment for *his* or *her* chemical dependence. Family members have worked hard to manage this problem, often trying to deny it or keep it a secret, and now they are asked to publicly walk into the building with the large sign, "Downtown Center for Alcohol and Other Drug Treatment." To many family members, going to treatment for this problem means going public with a shameful family secret.

This makes the therapist's work more difficult. The therapist must accept the user's defensiveness and denial, accept the family's feelings of vulnerability, shame, anger, and hopelessness, and at the same time, help them all take some tentative steps toward recovery. If that isn't enough, some family members will focus their anger and frustration directly on the therapist, sometimes by verbal attacks on the therapist's competence or person. Joining can be a large order in therapy with CD families.

If CD clients are referred by the courts, counselors have the upper hand. Joining doesn't seem so necessary; CD clients can either take what is offered or take the consequences. Early confrontation on a court referred CD client can be a tempting power play, especially for CD professionals who already have too many clients. With due respect toward these professionals, this leverage is often used too early. Court referrals are like having a big, legal claw hammer—one side to pry lose the resistance and denial, and if that doesn't work, another side to deliver the blow of reporting noncompliance. This leverage is always available, so why not just shelve it until it's clearly needed? Meanwhile, the counselor can practice the compassionate art of careful joining and become a more competent therapist.

With chemically dependent clients and their families, joining before confronting is essential. Confrontation will do little good until CD clients believe that the therapist is trying to understand them and help them make their life better. Until rapport is established and until they care about their relationship with the therapist, the confrontation has little power. The therapist is reduced to just another nagging, controlling goody-goody or another power-mad authority figure, who doesn't understand the IP, the family, or either's situation.

95

The most hostile or uncooperative member of a CD family often needs the most careful joining, especially if that member is a mother or father who is also the alcohol or other drug user and who has been coerced into treatment. Joining with this person may not be easy. Angry persons can be irritating, intimidating, and difficult. In a family session it's much more tempting to attend to the polite and suffering spouse and children than to the antagonistic and profane IP. But if the therapist consistently sides with the other family members by patronizing or ignoring the CD client's anger, it's only a matter of time before he or she will treat the therapist like one of them. Should this happen, the therapist has, in fact, joined the family system, but in a negative way that maintains the old pattern of "us against him or her." Therapists must find some way of taking IPs seriously without necessarily agreeing with their viewpoints, without lying to them, and without compromising their own integrity as therapists.

In situations like the one above, it helps to remember that for better or worse the IP is the parent for the children and always will be. My bedrock assumption is that the IP parent is a person who cares about his or her family no matter how he or she acts. The IP is in the tight grip of a disease whose hallmark is denial, with anger not far behind. Thus, the IP is generally far too busy defending himself or herself to be capable of clear thinking. It also helps to have observed many chemically dependent persons transcend this insanity and lose their facade of blaming, denial, and arm-swinging anger once they become serious about recovery. Such transformations are human marvels.

For effective joining with angry CD clients, it helps to replace irritation with curiosity. Become intrigued by this agitated person , how he or she got that way, and how he or she manages to maintain denial despite so much contrary evidence. When the therapist finds even the most hostile people interesting and tries to understand them better, he or she will naturally approach them in more acceptable ways. More than that, the therapist will see them as offering a unique opportunity to explore the baffling phenomenon of massive denial.

During difficult joining times, tell yourself, "Try to be patient. Reach around the chemical dependence and touch the person." The following little poem by Edward Markham also helps:

> He drew a circle that shut me out,
> Heretic, rebel, a thing to flout,
> But love and I had wit to win;
> We drew a circle that took him in.

Assigning Tasks

Tasks are between-session activities assigned to a family in order to introduce new experiences into the family's life, to provide information about family patterns and about possibilities for change, and to keep the family connected to the therapist between sessions.

Tasks have many uses, depending on the immediate goal of the therapist. One example is to begin rebuilding relationships between members. A recovering mother could be asked to take her daughter to a shopping mall or to engage in some other activity the two would enjoy together. A recovering teenager could plan to take younger siblings to a movie, while the parents enjoy a quiet evening at home. A recovering parent could take a child to the bank to open his or her first savings account.

Clarifying parent-child boundaries is another use for tasks. A favorite task is to ask the mother and father to have a date, the way they used to when they were courting; the children, of course, would not be included. This task points out that the husband and wife have a relationship with each other that is, in many ways, independent of the children. It's surprising how seldom parents make time for each other as a couple, and how frequently they admit that they haven't been out together in years.

Reestablishing role modeling for a recovering parent is another use for tasks. A recovering father, for example, could be asked to teach his son about cooking by fixing a meal with him for the family. A recovering mother could help her grade-school daughter with her homework for two or three nights during the week between therapy sessions.

Tasks should be kept simple and relatively easy, especially at first. Pick a task that is likely to be successful to give the family a good start in therapy. For a couple with communication problems around a particular topic, don't assign the task of discussing the issue together for an hour during the coming week. That's usually too difficult. Remember that relationships in recovery can be uncomfortable and awkward at first. I once assigned a task to a recovering father and his nine-year-old son to go fishing together. The son was excited about the day-long outing and the father agreed that it would be fun. Several weeks later, after three unsuccessful attempts at the outing, I finally asked the father why the fishing trip never occurred. "I'm not about to sit in a boat with my boy for three hours; we don't have that much to say." What seemed to me like a pleasant activity together was too difficult for them.

Make a specific plan with the family for the activity: who, what, where, and when. "Doing something together next week" is not a task; it's just a vague intention. If father and daughter agree to attend a movie together, which movie will they pick? What day and time? What will the mother and the other children do during that time? If they miss the movie on Tuesday evening, can they make it Thursday? When agreeing on tasks, encourage them to pin down the details together, and ask questions to be sure that all the specifics are covered.

Whenever possible, start the task in the session. During one session, for example, the parents agreed that the father would take over the discipline of their eight-year-old daughter for a week to give the mother a rest. When the parents were asked to begin the task in the session by talking with each other about what to do if the daughter became a problem, the mother started coaching the father on exactly how to discipline the child ("no loud words, no hitting, no squeezing, use only verbal persuasion; do not show anger—it upsets her"). It was obvious that the mother was not able to trust the father to deal with the daughter his way. This exercise proved that the task was too advanced and assigned too early. Starting the task in the session also led to a productive exploration of this important block in the couple's parenting.

It is usually a good idea to assign everyone in the family a role in the task. On a mother-father date, for example, the children could agree to remind the parents the day before the date so they won't "forget." On the father-son cooking task, the other members can agree to clean up afterwards. Assigning everyone a role in the task makes it a family commitment.

After the family plans the activity, ask, "How can the plan fail?" Someone will usually tell you. During one session a seven-year-old daughter answered the question: "It won't work because Daddy will never do it. He thinks it's silly to do things like that." After more exploration, the family came up with a different and more appropriate activity.

Finally, the task should be discussed early in the next session: "How was the movie, outing, date, etc.?" If tasks are not brought up by the therapist, a family will not take them seriously. If the assignment wasn't completed, or only done partially, discuss it thoroughly, since an uncompleted task gives valuable information about who cooperates with whom and how the family functions together. Exploring uncompleted tasks can reveal as much information as discussing completed ones.

It's important to make tasks important to the family. If family members haven't completed a task for the previous week, talk about it thoroughly at the beginning of the session: "You seemed so willing to do that. What happened?" If the excuses are legitimate, and sometimes they are, assign the task again. If the excuses are not legitimate, don't let them do that task again: "You passed by that opportunity; maybe we can think of another activity." Through all this, the family gets the impression that tasks are important to the therapy and to the therapist.

With active, results-oriented families, tasks can be used earlier than with families in which the recovering members appear unable to tolerate even a small change during early sobriety. In some families, it is appropriate to assign tasks between the first and second session; with others, not until after two or three sessions. The guide, as always, is the clinical judgment of the therapist concerning the readiness of the family members for change.

Tasks give the therapy an active, real-life flavor, and send the message that doing different leads to feeling different. Even when the tasks don't have their intended result, the therapeutic message lingers.

Creating Enactments

As therapists, when we talk with an individual member during a family session, we can easily believe the member is talking only to us. This is an illusion. Family members measure what they say and how they say it as a message to other members who are present. They are always talking to each other, regardless of who they're looking at when they speak.

The relative safety of a family member telling the therapist *about* someone rather than talking directly to that person is valuable because it offers objectivity to both speaker and listeners. But at some point, it is also valuable for family members to encounter each other with their communication difficulties and other issues. Enactments are the therapeutic tools with which to accomplish this.

Enactments are conversations during therapy sessions between two or more family members about one of their relevant issues. The therapist sets up the conversation or allows it to happen. These interactions provide a safe, structured environment for the members to deal with each other on important topics. They also shift the therapist's position from one of communication "switchboard" to a less central role in the family communication. This gives the therapist and family a direct opportunity to explore and change communication habits and patterns between and among members.

Enactments set up the conditions for a family to do its own work, with the therapist as a guide. They are essential tools in strengthening the whole-family-message (discussed in Chapter 2) by keeping relationships, rather than individuals, the central focus for therapy. Enactments allow the therapist to structure the communication during the session so that members can take responsibility for making their own decisions and working through their own issues.

Many family members are unsure about what they are supposed to do in therapy and depend on the therapist to set the rules. They may hesitate to talk directly to each other because the therapist is supposed to be the central figure. This was expressed by a couple whom I had asked to talk with each other instead of to me about a particular issue. After the conversation they thanked me for being allowed to do this: "Our previous therapist didn't want us to talk to each other in the sessions. I guess he was uncomfortable with arguments and conflict. We have our disagreements, but we are capable of talking together as two adults." Occasionally, therapists need to be reminded that families have managed to survive a long time without them.

What does the therapist do while the participants are talking together? Remember, the therapist is still involved, but on a different level. Instead of being an active participant in the conversation, the therapist is now an observer, encouraging direct communication between members. The therapist's role during enactments is to listen with ears and heart.

The therapist, as observer, is receiving information about relationships—who is close, who is distant, who is in conflict or disagreement—and about communication styles, strengths, weaknesses, and problem-solving ability. And, from a non-central position, the therapist is also sending the message that the family members must work together to change their relationships. The therapist can help family members change their relationships, but he or she can't do it for them.

Many enactments are used to coach and support the participants toward more effective communications: "I know this is difficult for you, but you are talking well together" or "That point may be a little hazy. Can you clarify that with him?" or "It seems like you want to say more than you're saying to each other" or "She doesn't appear to fully understand what you mean."

If one of the therapeutic goals is to interrupt enmeshment and enabling, an enactment can be very useful. An enabling father who is overinvolved with his CD son could be asked to sit aside with the therapist and listen to his wife and son talk about a certain topic—the son's behavior at home, school work, or other subject that fits the situation. In an instance like this, it is beneficial for the enmeshed father to see that the mother and child have a relationship that is, in some ways, independent of him. The therapist lends support to help the father stay out of the conversation.

In enactments, the therapist acts as a catalyst to the conversation, not as a participant. The enactment keeps the focus on the family members, with the therapist only punctuating and commenting on certain aspects of their dialogue. For example, in an enactment between spouses, the therapist might say, "I see your wife nodding her head, but I'm not convinced she agrees"; or, to parents, "See if you can keep your son from interrupting while you are deciding this together." The therapist may also want to include others in an enactment between two members: "What is your opinion in this conversation between your wife and daughter?" During all this, family members are practicing direct communication with each other and learning firsthand about how the others feel and think.

Clearly, the most important purpose of enactments is to keep the focus on the family. Enactments help families avoid the subtle shifting of responsibility to the therapist for "fixing" the identified patient or other problematic family member. Extensive one-on-one counseling between the therapist and CD member during a family session allows— more often, forces—the family members to step aside and let the therapist work with the problem person. In a family session, this is not productive for several reasons: it promotes an individual view of the

CD problem and makes the other members feel unnecessary; it gives far too much power and responsibility to the therapist; and, during the "individual" counseling, the relationships between and among the other family members go unnoticed.

Because enactments focus on the family, they also strengthen family connections. The therapist can say to a wife: "Your husband hasn't expressed his opinion about that. Find out from him what he thinks." Here the therapist is modeling what must happen in the family's real life—communicating, actively involving each other, and asking questions rather than making assumptions about a person's thoughts and feelings. Another interesting enactment that helps to strengthen relationships and to draw clearer boundaries between family members is to have two or more siblings talk to each other on a relevant topic while the parents listen. I once asked two teenage brothers to talk together about how the younger brother's drug use had affected the relationship between them. An intense dialogue followed, exposing for the first time the anger, disappointments, and love between the brothers. The parents were listening raptly, as if in a trance. I am intrigued at the novelty of this transaction in many families—the parents have never observed their teenagers having a serious conversation with each other, exploring their sibling relationship independent of the parents.

Enactments also can be used to establish parental authority and teamwork. A therapist could say to the parents: "To be clear with your son, decide together now what the two of you will do if he comes home late again. I will listen while you talk together." In this example the therapist is encouraging the parents to do in the session what they must do at home—communicate and plan with each other the limits and consequences for one of their children's behaviors. If the negotiation between the parents becomes difficult or lengthy, the therapist should ask the parents' permission for the children to leave the room. Once they agree on the issue at hand, the children or the involved child can be brought back in, and the parents can share what they decided.

Enactments can be used to help one or more children negotiate with their parents. To a CD adolescent, a therapist might say, "Tell your parents what it will take for them to get off your back. I will move out of your way while you talk." This enactment gets the therapist out of the middle, allowing for direct communication between parents and child; it also gives much information about relationships. Or, to support a young person in his or her negotiation with parents for something the child wants, a therapist might say, "Your mom and dad have said no to your request. Find out from them under what conditions they will say yes." Make clear, however, that the final decision always rests with the parents, not with the therapist or the child.

Sometimes it's necessary for the therapist to shift position in the room to encourage enactments. This clearly signals that the family members need to talk to each other, not to the therapist. Without a physical shift—looking away from them, moving back the chair, standing, or moving to another part of the room—families will tend to keep the therapist in the conversation, preferring to tell him or her something about a family member rather than telling that person directly.

Finally, remember that enactments must be relevant to the family members' concerns. Therapists who try to create enactments between members by requesting, "find out from her how she feels about that" may discover that the person has not been concerned because he or she already knew how the other felt. Find out what members know and care about first. Ask questions such as, "Do you know how she sees that?" or "Have you talked about this before?" or "Do you think she agrees with that plan?" If the answer is no, then suggest, "Check this out with her now so you can be sure."

Segmenting

Segmenting is the technique that divides the family into smaller groups for a particular purpose. A family can be segmented during the session, as when young children are assigned activities in another part of the room while the therapist talks with the parents. Or the therapist could ask the parents' permission for the children to wait in the reception area while the therapist talks with the parents about areas of family functioning that are not part of the children's responsibility, such as a decision the parents must reach together, exploring the parents' marital or sexual relationship, or looking into their relationships with in-laws.

Segmenting is more dramatic and powerful than are enactments in drawing boundaries around relationships in a family. In the above examples, segmenting makes a statement about the different role responsibilities of parents and children, namely, that some issues simply are not the children's business.

This boundary-making is often necessary in CD families, especially with adolescents or young adults who have taken on many of the decision-making responsibilities of the parents, often setting their own curfews, dictating their own use of automobiles in the family, deciding whether they will work part-time to earn their spending money, and deciding other issues that affect the safety and security of the family. In such cases, the adolescent is in charge, and this reversed parent-child hierarchy usually produces problems. Most teenagers don't have the maturity or life experience to make good decisions about the family, especially if the teenager is thinking with a brain affected by alcohol or other drugs.

Segmenting may also be necessary in family sessions to remove the distraction of younger children whose attention spans prevent them from being a part of the adult conversation. There is no point in allowing children to disrupt a family session, hooking everyone, including the therapist, into managing their behavior, and thus allowing little or nothing to be achieved during the session. Instead, it's better to place the children in the care of a colleague, or to take them to the corner of the room to do some drawings (see Chapter 5 for examples), or to remove them to the waiting area under the supervision of an older sibling or grandparent, or simply to omit them from the next session.

Before segmenting a child out of a session, however, it is important to see how the family handles the child's behavior. Does one of the parents attempt to do all the disciplining? Which parent is strict and which is lenient? How far are the child's disruptions allowed to go before a parent steps in? In one family, a four-year-old child was fond of removing books from the shelf in my office. His recovering single-parent mother had a higher tolerance for my scattered books than I did. I finally got a firm grip on the obvious and said, "Your son appears to be removing my books from the shelf. I like them where they are. Would you please get Tommy to stop doing that?" She did, but Tommy moved next to the potted plants in the window, digging with his tiny fingers into the black dirt. Another statement about his little hands scattering the soil around my office prompted the mother to action. In addition to saving my office, these interactions gave me a chance to observe this mother being a mother.

Segmenting can also give the therapist more power, a common need in therapy with CD families. If entrenched coalitions in the family make it difficult to maneuver among its hidden politics, ask for brief separate interviews: "I often do this routinely, knowing that you may have things that you are uncomfortable saying with the whole family present." When the whole family reconvenes, the therapist is the only one to have talked with everyone privately. This gives the therapist the power that comes from having the most information.

If the therapist believes that the family has a destructive secret, which loyalty or fear prevents the members from revealing, it's a good idea to segment the members into two or more separate interviews, lasting about 15-20 minutes each. The therapist might have separate interviews with each parent and another with the children, for a total of three interviews during a one-hour session. Precede each separate interview with, "I am not free to reveal anything you say to your family unless I believe that someone might be in danger." Whenever segmenting for this purpose, it's best to bring the family members back together briefly before they leave to give them support and encouragement and to make a few general comments about the family's problem situation. To prevent undue paranoia or suspicions of side-taking, it is also best to keep the times for each interview approximately equal.

Separate interviews can be used if the therapist senses dangers in the family but can't bring them out in the conjoint session. Such dangers might include suspected sexual, physical, or emotional abuse of children, wife battering, or other types of violence within the family. In the case of suspected violence, the topic during the separate sessions should revolve around the question "Are you afraid of anyone in the family getting hurt?" In the case of sexual abuse, have a same-sex colleague interview the possible victim. After these interviews, and if the sexual abuse is confirmed or still suspicious, first discuss the case thoroughly with a colleague to be sure you're thinking straight about it, and then comply with the law and notify the Department of Social Services, informing the parents that therapists are required by law to report any suspicion that a child may be physically or emotionally harmed in a family. Such a move may not endear the parents to the therapist, but it is preferable to suspecting something but doing nothing.

Segmenting can be used when arranging for the next session. For example, the therapist can tell the parents: "Next time I would like to see just the two of you, so we can talk about your decisions about the rules of the house for your daughter." Before doing this sort of segmenting, however, the therapist needs some understanding of the family relationships. For example, in the above situation such segmenting might not be the best idea if the daughter is strongly influential in the family and does not like being excluded from the session. If this is the case, she may be persuasive enough to talk the parents out of returning. Most young people, however, are delighted if they don't have to attend the next session.

Another precaution about not inviting someone to the next session: Don't leave out the CD member too early. I once made the mistake of inviting only the parents of the young adult CD client back to the second session, only to have the father soundly berate me for leaving out "the one who's causing all the trouble." The father had a point—I had prematurely taken the focus off the IP and placed it on the parenting relationship.

~~~~~~~

Joining, assigning tasks, creating enactments, and segmenting are essential therapy techniques for a brief, active, goal-directed model of therapy. These techniques help the therapist to become proactive—not just reactive—in providing change experiences for the family. More than that, they can make therapy more active and interesting for family and therapist alike.

Chapter 5

Additional Techniques

The techniques outlined in the previous chapter are fundamental to working with family dynamics. They are not, however, the only ones needed by the therapist. This chapter describes other techniques that can add both flexibility and precision to the therapist's interventions.

Some of the family therapy techniques in this section are old standbys and have been achieving good results for years. In this category are Sculpting, Alter Ego, Circular Questions, Reframing, and Drawings. Others I have originated, for example, Brief Network Intervention, New Talk, Safe Rebellion, and Guardrail.

From a clinical standpoint, techniques have several advantages. They compress much information and behavior into a short period of time, an important consideration in a brief model of therapy. Circular Questions and Sculpting, for example, can provide the therapist with a picture of the family patterns much more quickly than a rambling verbal description by family members. Techniques can also add variety and novelty to an interview, offering alternatives to the "sit down and talk" modality. Movements, drawings, and experiential exercises are active metaphors through which family members can communicate feelings and thoughts. Finally, techniques offer a clear framework for the family members and for the therapist during nervous exploration of emotional and ambiguous issues in the family's life. The structure and ground rules of techniques like Alter Ego and

New Talk reduce the confusion and resistance that usually accompany new behavior.

Techniques can also have disadvantages. If a therapist applies a procedure when it's not appropriate, he or she is laying a template over family members and insisting they arrange themselves to fit. A technique is not appropriate when it distracts the family from an issue that members consider important, or when it pushes them to do something they aren't ready for, or when it doesn't match the family's tempo or mood. As soon as the therapist discovers that a technique is out of place, it's best to drop it and try another approach.

Neither can technique in therapy replace compassion, sincerity, and warmth. Too much reliance on technique promotes the idea that a family is an object to be acted upon—a one-way process of maneuvering the family with a structured, mechanistic procedure, making the therapist a detached technician, who gives little or nothing of himself or herself in the encounter.

A final disadvantage in using techniques has to do with manipulation. Is the family simply but cleverly being tricked into doing what the therapist wants them to do? This is a vexing ethical question in any type of therapy, but I have come to believe that it is impossible *not* to manipulate people in therapy. Almost every message, gesture, nod, and movement—consciously or unconsciously—is an attempt by the therapist to increase certain client responses and decrease others. If manipulation is defined as artful control in pursuit of the family's goals and as skillful management of the sessions to reach these goals, then therapy is manipulation, and so are techniques.

For me, the ethical question is, "For whose benefit am I doing this?" If I use techniques to manipulate families to fulfill my own ego needs or esthetic preferences, then therapy becomes self-serving and ineffective. As a therapist, I have been guilty of intruding too much into a session, showing off with quick salesman-like responses and rapid strategic moves. Through experience, I have learned to carefully monitor the family's response to a technique and to use the family's feedback to determine whether I am working on an agenda that is important to the family and to the treatment, or on one that is just personally important to me.

This chapter includes some of the more reliable and comfortable therapeutic tools I have used for CD family therapy. They have all been taught to other CD family therapists. I've tried to write each one clearly enough so it can be read and applied at the next appropriate opportunity or briefly enough to quickly review prior to a session. These techniques work best when they are selected and modified to fit the unique therapeutic situation and when the therapist adapts them comfortably to his or her own personality and style.

Alter Ego

Definition and Purpose

With permission, the therapist sits behind a family member and speaks for him or her. This technique can be used to:
1. Increase the intensity of feelings in the room.
2. Prompt the family to deal with an important issue that is being avoided.
3. Explore how one or more family members are feeling or thinking.
4. Encourage more participation from a silent member.

Procedure

1. Instructions: "I want to try something which may appear silly, but bear with me. I would like to talk for Bob. Is that okay with you, Bob? I will sit behind you and let your family pretend that you are talking instead of me. If I say anything you disagree with, please correct me."
2. The therapist then puts a chair behind Bob (or sits on the floor) *out of direct eye contact* with the family. This creates the illusion that Bob, not the therapist, is talking.

111

3. The therapist can start the conversation by picking up on a current topic or by saying, "You may want to begin by asking Bob some questions about how he is thinking or feeling. I will answer for him."

4. If the family member stops the "Alter Ego" therapist to make a correction ("That's not the way I feel/think"), let the person speak for himself or herself; then continue as Alter Ego.

Case Example

The family consisted of mother, father, and two sons, ages 17 and 19. The youngest son was in inpatient treatment for chemical dependence. The session revealed that he had been using cocaine and marijuana for three years without his parent's knowledge. He had devised a number of tricks for deceiving his parents and was not detected until he was arrested for possession of drugs. The Alter Ego technique was used to dramatize the son's deception and cleverness with the parents and to warn the parents that their son could continue to use drugs while convincing everyone that he was recovering.

After getting permission, the therapist sat behind the son and spoke as his Alter Ego. Before starting, the therapist said, "If I say anything you don't agree with, please correct me. If you don't correct me, we will assume you agree." At the beginning of the exercise, a few non-threatening warm-up remarks were made back and forth before this conversation began:

Alter Ego: Mom and Dad, I know you love me, but you also scare me. You scare me because when I get out of this hospital I could go back to drugs and you wouldn't even know it.
Dad: I believe we would, Son.
Alter Ego: Well, I fooled you for a long time.

Mother: Yes, but that was before we understood what chemical dependence was all about.

Alter Ego: So you think you know enough now to catch me? I think I can still fool you.

Dad: It hurts for you to think we would be that stupid.

Alter Ego: Do you blame me for being worried about it?

Dad: Don't you worry, we plan to pay close attention this time.

Pointers for the Therapist

1. This technique should not be tried until some rapport and trust is established between the therapist and family (at about the third or fourth family session).

2. The therapist does not just roleplay the member, saying only what he or she would say. The power of this techniques is that it allows the therapist to gently bring up important feelings and thoughts of which the member is unaware or about which he or she is afraid to speak.

3. Start in a relatively non-threatening way. Don't get deep into feelings and emotional issues until the family adjusts to the game.

4. Don't go too fast. Leave pauses and gaps to allow the family to absorb what's being said.

5. Variation: Speak for a few minutes for one member, then shift to another member. With each member repeat the instructions, "Please correct me if I say anything you disagree with." If the member stops you ("That's not the way I feel or think"), let the person speak for himself or herself, then continue as Alter Ego.

6. Double Alter Ego: Ask a colleague to join you for a session; after allowing 20-30 minutes for the colleague to get to know the family, each therapist can be the Alter Ego of a different family member simultaneously, carrying on a dialogue between the Alter Egos. Again, don't go too fast.

Brief Network Intervention (BNI)

When trying to help chemically dependent individuals and families out of their rigid patterns, strong and sudden leverage is sometimes needed, especially for clients and families who have restabilized after the initial crisis that got them to seek treatment. The Brief Network Intervention can provide that leverage.

Definition and Purpose

The chemically dependent client, his or her significant others, and relevant professionals are brought together in a meeting to help the client avoid a serious mistake or future harm. The immediate goal is to prevent an impending negative behavior by the CD client, such as dropping out of treatment, running away from home, losing a job, violating probation, or continuing to drive while impaired. A broader goal is to change enabling patterns at the family or professional network level that may be contributing to the problem.

Procedure

The family therapist calls a meeting of the CD client and the people who are involved in his or her life. Anyone who has influence can be invited: nuclear and extended family, treatment staff who have clinical or administrative influence, probation officers, social workers, school counselors, minister, roommate, friend. One and a half to two hours should be allowed for the session.

The professionals involved with the case are contacted in advance by the family therapist and informed about the goal of the meeting. Example: "Tammy is continuing to use drugs while in treatment in our adolescent program. Before reporting this violation to her juvenile probation officer, we want to arrange a meeting with you and her family and other professionals to confront her drug use and try to keep her out of the juvenile detention center. Will you help?"

Once everyone is assembled, the family therapist acts as moderator,

114

beginning by asking each person about his or her involvement with the CD client or family and his or her view of the problem situation. The therapist then clarifies the goal: to help the CD client avoid a specific act that would probably cause harm to the client or to someone else. *How will each person react* if the client engages in the destructive behavior? The therapist keeps the meeting focused on the goal, coordinates input from the group, clarifies, and moves the group toward a specific plan of action.

Case Example

Denny, a sixteen-year-old son in a blended family, was in outpatient treatment for alcohol and other drug use and on probation for stealing. The BNI was held to prevent him from being expelled from treatment for poor attendance. Present at the session were Denny, his mother and stepfather, the natural father, two younger half siblings, the family therapist, group therapist, supervisor of the treatment program, and his probation officer.

It soon became evident to Denny, and to everyone else, that unsuccessful completion of treatment would have far-reaching consequences for the young man. In response to the question, "How will you react if Denny drops out of treatment?" the mother and stepfather said they would not allow Denny to remain at home if he left treatment; the natural father did not offer refuge for the boy if he left home; the family therapist and program supervisor said that if Denny was absent from group treatment once more, they would recommend inpatient treatment; the probation officer said he would take the case back to the judge if Denny violated probation by leaving treatment prematurely.

Denny was squirming during the session. His escape from treatment was blocked by the tight cooperation of his family and professional network. At the same time, he also learned of everyone's concern for him, especially from his natural father, who traveled several hundred miles to attend, and who Denny thought didn't care. Denny saw that his family and several professionals were taking the time to attend this meeting and to state their limits on his behavior. He reluctantly decided to stay in treatment, which he successfully completed several weeks later.

Comments

A BNI has several positive effects. It can:
1. Increase the teamwork and coordination among professionals and significant others, thus weakening the "divide and conquer" strategies of some CD clients.
2. Catalyze change; more change can be generated in one BNI than in several individual, group, or family sessions.
3. Result in a clear direction and plan for the CD client, family, and professional staff.
4. Save time by eliminating separate conversations, therapy sessions, and meetings with the various subgroups involved in the CD client's case.

A BNI is a therapeutically arranged crisis that takes advantage of two well-known phenomena: (1) the breakdown of rigid patterns of behavior is more likely during a crisis than during periods of stability; and (2) a person's significant network of others is a powerful motivator for change. A BNI meeting usually turns into a mixture of love and concern on the one hand, and a "show of force" on the other. The therapist has compassion and respect for the CD client's and the family's dilemma, but there is also a sense of urgency—certain behaviors will be met with serious consequences.

The BNI is similar to the Johnson Institute Family Intervention, but it differs in that the BNI:
1. Requires no rehearsal or preparation except for the initial phone calls to invite the participants.
2. Casts a broader net: a client's family, social, *and* treatment network are all targets for change in how they have been reacting to the client's problem behaviors.

116

3. Has more uses than the Family Intervention, which is usually limited to getting a CD client and/or family into a treatment or recovery program.

A BNI can be used with any potentially harmful behavior where strong leverage and influence is needed quickly for a specific purpose. Besides preventing someone from leaving CD treatment prematurely, I have used the BNI to help runaway teenagers return home, to avoid a CD client's mental hospital commitment, to get a chemically dependent adult into treatment instead of jail, to help a chemically dependent single mother enter treatment in order to regain custody of her children, and to help end the dangerous drug-related behavior of a teenage girl who was reacting to her parent's divorce.

Not all of the above BNI's achieved their intended purpose, but they were all productive. During the meetings change was in the air. Whatever the outcome of the session, the CD client, family, and professional network felt the pressure to find new solutions. After the BNI, they do not deal with their particular problem in the same way they did before.

Circular Questions

Definition and Purposes

Circular questions are those questions directed to a family member about relationships between and among *other* family members. This technique gives useful information because people will often make more objective observations if they are not directly involved. Concerning relationships other than our own, we all have some "armchair psychologist" in us.

The purposes of this technique are to:

1. Give the therapist a quick overview of the family structure, or to test a hypothesis about the family.
2. Give the family members information about other members' perceptions of the family.

3. Present the family to itself as a set of interacting relationships, not a collection of individuals acting independently.

Procedure and Examples

1. Instructions: "To get to know you better, I would like to ask several questions about relationships in your family. This will give us a better idea of how everyone is thinking. If I ask anything you would prefer not to answer, please say so."
2. Ask questions like the following:
   a. To a CD parent: "Which of your children do you believe is most worried about this problem, your son or your daughter?"
   b. To the other parent: "Who do you think pays more attention to your daughter's moods, your spouse or your son?"
   c. To a son: "If your mother got upset but tried to hide it, who would notice first, your sister or your father?"
   d. To a daughter: "Who is more strict with your brother, your mother or father?"
3. Answers to the questions often trigger conversations between family members. The therapist can pursue these if they seem productive.
4. Answers can be checked out with other family members ("Do you agree with that?").
5. Questions do not have to be evenly distributed among family members.

Drawings

Definition and Purposes

This is a technique in which family members draw (i.e., produce a likeness or representation) of their view of family relationships or of an event in the family's life. Drawings have several purposes:

1. They are especially useful with children who need a nonverbal way to express themselves.
2. They encourage each member to think about the family as an interacting unit instead of as individuals acting separately.
3. They reveal the part of each person's feelings, thoughts, and attitudes that is difficult to put into words. Many clients will draw what they are afraid to say.
4. Drawings are metaphors and are more complex and flexible than words. They get at the richness of our inner experience.
5. Drawings can give important information to the therapist and to the family. They can be saved and referred to later. They are a concrete object to focus on, to study, to revise, to accept or reject.
6. Drawings can be employed for strategic purposes:
   a. To mark parent-child boundaries in the family. For example, the children are instructed to work on the drawings in another part of the room or in a different room while the parents are talking with the therapist.
   b. To create motivation. The therapist finds in the drawings something to support the direction he or she wants the family to take; or finds unanswered questions in the drawings that need to be explored in therapy.

The following section offers several drawing exercises the therapist can use with families. After the drawings are completed and discussed in the session, the therapist can ask if he or she can keep the drawings. They then become part of the therapist's information about the family.

Family Circle Method *

1. Give each person a pencil and a sheet of unlined paper on which a large circle has been drawn.
2. Instructions: "Place your family on the paper. Use a smaller circle for each person. You can put them inside or outside the big circle. You can put them close together or far apart. And you can make them large or small."
3. Family members should not see each other's pictures while they are drawing.
4. When they finish, each person, in turn, places his or her picture on the floor in the center of the group so everyone can see the drawing and talk about it.
5. The therapist makes observations about each drawing, asks questions, and prompts discussion. Do not make interpretations; just make comments about the figures on the paper ("I notice that you put yourself closest to your father and put your sister closest to your mother").
6. When the discussions are over, ask the family members if you can keep their drawings. Put name, age, and date on each drawing and file them in the CD client's chart for later reference.
7. Variation: After the family members finish drawing, say, "Now turn the page over and draw it the way you *want* it to be." The differences in the two drawings could be taken metaphorically as the contract between the family member and the therapist. Allow discussion, as before.

---

* Susan M. Thrower, et. al., "The Family Circle Method for Integrating Family Systems Concepts in Family Medicine," *The Journal of Family Practice*, 15 (1982): 451-457.

Empty Room

1. Give everyone an unlined sheet of blank paper.
2. Instructions: "I want you to pretend that you are looking down on an empty room (the paper) with no furniture. Place your family in the room where they would be comfortable. Use a circle for each person."
3. All other procedures are the same as steps 3-6 in the Family Circle Method.

Family Picture

1. Move chairs out of the way to provide space; if appropriate, the family can sit on the floor to draw.
2. Provide crayons or colored pencils and *one* large sheet of blank paper, preferably a flip chart sheet or large poster paper.
3. Instructions to the whole family: "Draw a picture." If members ask for clarification of the instructions, reply, "Just draw a picture; you can do it any way you like."
4. Observe the process. Observe how the family decides what to do, who takes charge, who accommodates to whom, who talks the most or the least, etc.
5. When the family finishes, discuss the drawing. The therapist prompts the discussion and makes observations about the picture or the process of drawing together: "I see that three of you contributed to one picture, and one of you drew a separate picture," etc.

Family Relationships

1. This is usually more appropriate with only two persons (couple, parent-child, etc.) than with a whole family. Give each person an unlined sheet of paper.
2. Instructions: "Draw your relationship with each other." The family members should be allowed to interpret these instructions any way they choose.

3. Each person may include other people in his or her drawing.
4. When they finish, ask them to swap pictures. Then ask each person, "What do you see?" Encourage them to talk to each other about the drawings: to describe what's in the picture, to tell what it means to the person, to explain the message contained in it, etc.

Open House

1. This is more appropriate for children, ages 5-10. It can be done during a separate session with the children or given to them as a task while the therapist talks with the parents.
2. Instructions: "Pretend that you take the roof off your house and look down into the rooms. Draw the rooms in your house. Put your family in the house doing something. It's eight o'clock at night."
3. When they finish, encourage each child to show and explain his or her picture to the parents.
4. Discuss the picture to gain information about the family: the activities of each person in the picture, who was together in the same room, who was absent from the home, etc.

Draw-A-Dream

1. This is more appropriate with children (ages 5-16), and can be done without the parents being present.
2. Draw a rough sketch of a child sleeping in bed. Above it place a large cartoon balloon for the drawing.
3. Instructions: "This is a little girl (boy) sleeping in bed. She is having a bad dream. Draw the bad dream the girl (boy) is having."
4. When finished, ask the child to explain the dream and the figures in the drawing. Let the child make up a story about the drawing or just talk about it in any way he or she chooses.
5. Get the child's permission for his or her parents to see the picture and for you to talk to the parents about it.

Additional Drawing Exercises

Here are some additional possibilities for drawings. Others can be created in the moment to fit the situation. Supply paper and crayons or colored pencils and instruct the family members:

1. "Draw the problem as you see it."
2. "Draw how you would like the problem to change."
3. "Draw how it was in your family before the problem; during the problem; after the problem."
4. "Draw your relationship with your (mother, father, son, daughter)."
5. "Give a title to your drawing." (This can be used with any drawing.)
6. In Draw-a-Dream: "Draw a bad dream your (mother, father, sister, brother) is having."
7. "Draw something that shows how you feel about the family now."

New Talk

Definition and Purpose

In this technique, the therapist asks one family member to say something to another member he or she hasn't said before. The purpose of this technique is to break through to a new level of honesty in the family or to get beyond repetitive "analysis paralysis" of a particular issue. If a family member makes a new and important disclosure, it can be explored. A topic's importance does not depend on its content but on the emotion attached to it.

This technique is especially useful for advice-giving family members who repeatedly tell other members the same things. Such "do-right" lectures, although well-intentioned, are not beneficial because they have been repeated so many times.

Procedure and Examples

1. Instructions to a family member: "Will you take a small risk and try something with me? Say something to (name) that (he or she) hasn't heard you say to (him or her) before. I will get out of your way while you talk."

2. The therapist moves and sits closer to the talking member but out of direct eye contact. This removes the temptation for the talking member to draw the therapist into the conversation. It is also a position to lend support and encouragement if the request is difficult for the talker.

3. After the talking family member says something, ask the receiving member if what he or she heard was old or new. "Have you heard this before from (him or her)?" If the answer is yes, ask the talking member to try again.

4. Once the talking member says something new, the receiving member responds any way he or she chooses.

5. The therapist may need to gently block interruptions from other family members who try to change the subject or use distracting humor.

6. The therapist may want to reverse the roles by getting the receiving member to do the same thing with the talking member.

7. Variation: If the talking family member says only negative things to the receiving member, ask him or her to add something positive.

8. Variation: During a conversation between two family members (father and daughter, for example), ask the mother, "What do you see happening between your husband and daughter?" After the conversation, set up the New Talk technique. After it is completed, ask the mother again: "Now what did you see?"

9. Variation: Each family member can be asked to do the exercise: "Pick someone in your family and say something to him or her that you haven't said before."

Reframing

There are two types of Reframing: Problem Reframing and Positive Reframing.

Problem Reframing

Definition

The therapist offers a redefinition of a problem that shifts the family members' perspectives from an *individual* to a *family* level.

Examples

Problem	Reframe	Implied Action
"Our child is lazy and won't do what we say."	"under-responsible behavior"	Parents teach him responsibility.
"He won't talk to me or reveal how he feels."	"You want better communication with him."	Work on communication together.
"Our teenager is rebellious."	"She's doing her own thinking without benefit of the parents' help."	Get her to accept or listen to parents' thinking.

In the above examples the problem is that one person is behaving poorly and has a deficit or flaw that needs correcting. Thus, it is made to seem that the problem lies within one individual in the family. This is not an interactional, whole-family view of the difficulty. If this "frame" of the problem goes unchallenged, the family does not need to be present; individual therapy would be the proper treatment. The therapist's job is to find a way to include more than one person in the definition, to place the problem and the solution in a family relationship context. Family therapy then becomes the appropriate treatment. A good problem reframe does not distribute the blame for a problem. Rather, it makes everyone a part of the problem's solution.

Positive Reframing

Definition

A technique based on the assumption that for every negative thought, action, or feeling there is a positive intention or personal characteristic being expressed.

Statement	Reframe
(Client says)	(Therapist replies to the client)
"He never listens to me."	"It's clear that you want better communication with him."
"If people would just leave me alone, I would be all right."	"You like to do your own thinking and to take care of yourself."
"I'm going to leave treatment, and nobody can stop me."	"Once you make up your mind, you are very determined."
"There's nothing wrong with me. *They* have the problem."	"You are looking hard to find exactly where the problem lies."
"No matter how hard I try, I can't do better."	"Trying hard and doing better are obviously things you value."
"He's so stupid. He can't do anything right."	"It's plain to me that intelligent action is important to you."

A positive reframe is different from a reflection or an interpretation. For example, a CD client discloses, "Everybody is blaming me, but I think that others had a part in getting me fired from my job." A *reflection* gets at the here-and-now feelings behind the words, such as, "You seem to be angry about the way you were treated." An *interpretation* gets at the deeper meanings behind action or feelings, such as, "Could it be that you were looking for a way out of a job you really didn't like?" A *positive reframe* expresses the positive attribute or strength of the client being expressed by his or her statement, such as, "You obviously have the ability to take a hard look at painful situations to figure out what happened."

Pointers for Therapists

1. Say it affirmatively rather than as a question.
2. Say only what you believe.
3. Don't overuse reframing. Three times in a session is enough.
4. Don't argue with the person about your reframe.

Relabeling

Definition and Purpose

Relabeling is the use of benign words and phrases to replace disparaging labels used by family members to describe one another's behavior. The relabel, offered by the therapist, allows the therapist to refer to and discuss the behavior without offending the labeled member.

Description and Examples

At a workshop, a well-known family therapist played a videotape of a family in which the mother dominated the session. She corrected everyone, interrupting her husband and children to provide more detail, "clarification," or to reveal their hidden motives. The therapist turned off the tape and asked for a word or phrase to describe the mother. "She's a lawn mower," a participant answered. "No, no," the therapist replied. "She's a deep-sea diver!" The therapist's more benign relabel implied that the mother was one who sought more depth of understanding in the family interactions.

Here are some examples of common descriptive terms heard during family sessions (expletives deleted), and more neutral or benevolent substitutions.

Disparaging Label	Relabel
nagging	conscientious
jealous	passionate, loyal, devoted
overreactive	sensitive
sloppy	casual
aloof	rational
flighty	spontaneous
too strict	protective
confused	searching
nosey	curious
picky	thorough
scared	cautious

What we call things matters. Words contribute to the shape and feel of our experience. The essence of relabeling is to look at that part of the experience from a different angle, to walk to a new place.

Safe Rebellion

Definition and Purpose

Safe Rebellion is a technique in which the parents agree to stop trying to correct one of their recovering child's (usually an adolescent) annoying or "problem" behaviors. The purpose is to ease power struggles and conflicts between the parents and the teenager. This technique is used while the adolescent is successfully abstaining from alcohol or other drugs.

Many parents believe that adolescents do peculiar things—dress funny, wear their hair in odd ways, have sloppy personal habits, or use strange language. Often, parental values and preferences are violated, leading to much fighting, bickering, and tension between the parents and child, and between the parents themselves. The amount of anger and conflict, however, can be out of proportion to the importance of the behavior involved. The underlying issue is one of control. Safe Rebellion helps ease one or more of these conflicts by giving rule-setting power to the parents while, at the same time, giving control of the behavior to the son or daughter. This is consistent with the therapeutic direction of keeping the parents responsibly in charge of their adolescent.

Procedure

If the recovering adolescent and one or both parents had a pattern of fighting over the alcohol or other drug use, they often continue their conflicts and power struggles in other areas after the chemical use stops. Safe Rebellion can help in this situation. The technique requires the therapist to deliberately side with the parents to help them regain their rule-setting function in the home. The adolescent or other children in the family should not be present while the therapist is explaining the procedure to the parents.

First, some basic statements about normal adolescent development are made to the parents. For example, the therapist briefly explains the adolescent's need to rebel, to establish autonomy, to discover who he or she is, and to take control of himself or herself now that the alcohol or other drugs have stopped. These traits are healthy, normal, and expected. Parents usually accept these notions, at least intellectually.

The therapist then asks the parents to choose one of their adolescent's "rebellious" behaviors—such as his or her choice of music, clothes, or language—that the parents have unsuccessfully tried to correct or control but one that does not affect the health and safety of anyone in the home. If two parents are involved, they should talk to each other and agree on one behavior.

Once the behavior is chosen, the therapist sets the rules for the intervention: Parents are to continue expressing disapproval and annoyance at the adolescent's rebellious behavior but *make no attempt to change it.* If the opportunity arises, each parent, or the involved parent, is to make at least three negative comments during the coming week to the adolescent about the target behavior ("You're wearing *that* out in public?") but is not to try to correct it.

Case Example

A mother, divorced from her alcoholic husband, brought her fourteen-year-old daughter, Amy, to therapy complaining of her uncooperative behavior at home. The mother was distraught after several months of persistent and unsuccessful efforts to correct her daughter's personal hygiene, choice of clothes, friends, and reading material. During the assessment interview, the therapist sensed that Amy took secret delight in defeating her mother's overcontrolling attempts to correct her. The more Amy resisted her authority, the more the mother tried to correct and supervise, which resulted in more resistance. The typical parental moves of granting and removing privileges had not worked.

After several unsuccessful attempts to support the mother in regaining her authority, the therapist decided that a way was needed to unbalance the power struggle so that other relationship issues could be addressed. The therapist spoke with the mother alone, while Amy waited in the reception area. The therapist explained that some form of rebellion is normal during adolescence and that Amy was apparently better at rebellion than most teenagers. The therapist added that "the one who is really in control is the one who sets the rules of the game."

After some further discussion, the mother was willing to let Amy exercise her need to "defy the parent" if it did not affect the health and safety of anyone and if it resulted in less conflict in other areas. The mother was asked to choose something about Amy's habits, behavior, or activities that she had unsuccessfully tried to change but that she would be willing to let go. She picked the way Amy kept her room— disorganized, dirty clothes everywhere, stale food under the bed—that had been a point of conflict for the past year.

The therapist then set the task: the mother was to continue what she had been doing—expressing disgust and disbelief as she passed by Amy's room in a voice Amy could hear—at least three times during the coming week. The only difference was that this time she was *not* to try to get Amy to clean her room. The mother playfully practiced her "disapproving gestures" and statements during the session and agreed that the only reason she would take action would be if the mess created too many roaches or rats or if "something moldy and green" began growing into the hallway.

Within two weeks, the mother reported that she had carried out the task. "Amy is still no angel, but things are better between us." Amy added, "We don't fight as much." Using the technique of Safe Rebellion helped the mother and daughter relax some of the tension between them, moving therapy to a more central issue—the conflict between the divorced parents about Amy's visitation rights with the alcoholic father. Since the mother had complete legal custody of Amy, this problem was resolved by keeping the mother in charge of the visitation schedule and by supporting her efforts to resist being threatened by Amy with, "Father won't like this."

Comments

In this technique, the therapist joins with the parent to "put one over" on the adolescent. When the parent cooperates, this intervention becomes a playful, secretive teasing of the adolescent by the parent, and can ease some of the conflict that has accumulated over time. The parent regains control of the war by letting the adolescent win the battle.

At first, Safe Rebellion appears to violate the young person's rights in family therapy by allowing the therapist to enter into a secret coalition with the parent(s) against the child. However, we must remember that the therapist is really negotiating with the parents on the *child's* behalf. Also, everyone in the home benefits by the easing of tensions around one of the conflict topics in the family. The therapy moves along, bolstered by the parent's success in making a decision, taking action, and getting results.

Exercises Requiring Movement

Definition and Purpose

Movement exercises are the physical arrangement of family members in a way that symbolizes relationships in the family at a particular time. They add novelty and action to the therapy, leaving for a moment the well-traveled highway of words.

Classical Sculpting

1. Move chairs out of the way before starting. Ask everyone to stand.
2. Instructions: (To one family member): "Imagine that you're a sculptor and that your family is made of clay. Make a sculpture of your family. You can place them anywhere, in any position (illustrate with hands-on demonstration), and they must stay in that position like a statue. Show me what your family looks like to you. Be sure to put yourself in the picture."

3. While the family is sculpted in place, ask questions and make observations:
   a. (of each person): "How does it feel for you in this picture?"
   b. "Does this picture of the family surprise anyone?"
   c. "This appears to be a close family" or "Everyone's picture is so different (so similar)" or "The children have a different picture than the parents," etc.
4. It is sometimes best to ask a child to be the first sculptor. Children are more willing to "play," which provides a warm-up for the other family members.
5. Model physical touching while explaining procedure; be animated and active.
6. Use chairs or other objects to represent absent people.
7. Make sure everyone gets a turn.
8. Optional (to sculptor): "Now show me how you would *like* it to be."
9. Optional: "Let's do this without talking."

Picture the Problem

1. This exercise is a variation of Classical Sculpting.
2. Instructions (to one member): "Sometimes I understand pictures better than words. Show us a picture of the problem situation as you see it. Place people so that they fit into the picture. Give each person in your family something to do or say. I want to see how the problem looks."
3. Other observations and comments are similar to classical sculpting above.

Most/Least

1. Instructions (to each person, one at a time): "Arrange your family in a line according to who is most and who is the least worried about the situation. This part of the room will be the most worried and that part the least worried. Let's do this without talking."

2. Examples of content:
   a. Who *talks* the most/least?
   b Who *protects* others the most/least?
   c. Who is *strict* the most/least?
   d. Who is the most/least *powerful*?
3. Variation: Ask the whole family to do the exercise together: "Without talking, arrange yourselves according to who . . . (a, b, c, d above)."

Change the Distance

1. The therapist moves out of the family circle while giving instructions.
2. Instructions (while couple or family is sitting): "I want to ask you to do something which may appear silly, but bear with me. Change the distance between you." (Don't explain the instructions—they are clear enough.)
3. After they move, talk about what happened. Begin by asking everyone, "What did you see?"
4. Make observations about who moved first and last, who moved closer or farther away, and about small behaviors such as pauses, gestures, glances, and laughter.
5. By making comments, the therapist is creating metaphors about family relationships, using the family's own movements. Examples:
   a. "I noticed that everyone waited for mother to move first, then positioned themselves according to where she went."
   b. "The daughter is the only one who stayed firm where she was."
   c. "Father moved closer to the children."
   d. "When one person moved, everyone had to shift."
6. Allow any discussion the family would like. Often, this exercise will be the catalyst that brings up other relationship issues.

Place Yourself

1. When two or more members are talking to each other on a relevant topic, turn to another member and say: *"Place* yourself in this conversation. Show me where you are in this."
2. The therapist is looking for a physical response, not a verbal one.
3. Talk about what happened.

Guardrail

This is an appropriate technique to use with a family in which an adolescent or young person is the CD member and in which there are two parents or parent figures. Guardrail helps the therapist to bring both parents together as a team to react to the child's alcohol or other drug problem.

1. Introductory comments to the parents: "When you join together, support each other, and continue to work as a team, it provides clear limits to your child. It's like a strong guardrail lining a tall bridge you're crossing in a car—you hope you never touch the rail or even go near it, but it's comforting to have it there. You know it will keep you from going over the side, even if there was an accident."
2. Instructions: "To make this point, I want to ask you to do something. Join hands. To make the bond even stronger, move your hands up each other's arm and clasp the other's forearm." (Illustrate by clasping your forearms with opposite hands.)
3. While they are joined: "This is the kind of mutual support you will need from each other to set clear limits for your child. One of you may temporarily weaken, but as long as the other is holding firm, the guardrail is in place. While you are joined this way your child sees his or her boundaries and limits. Your child knows that if he or she goes beyond the limits you have set, you will take action together."

4. To the child: "Will you push on the guardrail to test its strength? Push on it to get its feel." (When this is done, the guardrail will give a little, but remain in place.) "The guardrail is flexible but it's also strong and solid."

5. This exercise fixes the idea of the parents' togetherness and teamwork in setting limits for their child. If appropriate, the parents should maintain the guardrail for a minute or so, while the therapist makes other remarks: "How can your child be sure the guardrail is in place?" "How can he or she get past the guardrail—go under or over it without your knowing?" "What would make one of you loosen your grip?" "Who is likely to loosen his or her grip first?"

~~~~~~~~~~

Therapists are encouraged to experiment with the techniques in this chapter. Usually these techniques accomplish their intended purpose, but regardless of the outcome, no therapeutic action with families is totally wasted, since active techniques are valuable for learning about the family's strengths, weaknesses and relationship patterns. Techniques are a way to get to know the family, making subsequent interventions more on target.

Most of the techniques in this chapter provide fun and play during treatment. They often bypass the verbal, rational, analytic, levels of understanding and enter the more varied and colorful world of analogy, metaphor, and expressive movement. Some levels of understanding can be reached more readily when people are in a more creative, loose, and playful mood. In fact, some family dynamics are just too uncomfortable to the family members to be reached in any other way. In therapy, serious issues are frequently reached through playful means.

Chapter 6

Traps and Tips

Some chemical dependence counselors still may use an individual, medical model of the disease as their only conceptual guide, and with it, a few related assumptions: (1) Chemical dependence is a compulsive disorder affecting an individual; (2) Like any compulsive disorder, it is treated individually; (3) With one chemical dependent in the family, there is one identified patient in the home; and (4) Once the chemical use stops, the client's family becomes stable. These assumptions are a place to start, but they are only a piece of a larger picture. Chemical dependence resides in the person and in the social network of which that person is a part. Chemical dependence is an interactional, as well as an individual, disease process.

This chapter discusses four traps therapists may encounter when first changing from an individual to a family systems approach in treating chemical dependence.

1. Focusing on the individual instead of the system
2. Getting bogged down in induction
3. Switching the problem person
4. Flying solo

All of these traps, either directly or indirectly, represent failures to recognize and use the interactional power of the family and the immediate social context in treating chemical dependence.

The first part of this chapter will discuss the four traps frequently encountered in CD family therapy, along with tips for avoiding them.

The second part will offer specific suggestions for the therapist to maintain a systems orientation through his or her manner of communicating with the families during the sessions.

This systems-based style of communicating will further reduce the pitfalls of these common traps.

TRAP 1: *Focusing on the Individual Instead of the System*

On an intellectual level, the systemic concept of a CD family achieving a dynamic, interdependent balance in its relationships is not especially difficult to understand. On a practicing level, however, a therapist can easily become trapped in an individual orientation to therapy during a family session. Most professionals who work with CD problems were trained in individual therapy, and they are comfortable with it. In fact, many tend toward individual, one-on-one therapy even during a session with a family; they tend to see the unit of treatment as the individual members, not the family. Many therapists who are new to the systems orientation see the separate petals, not the flower. Viewing the individual as only a part of a larger whole requires a shift in perspective.

Using enactments, discussed in Chapter 4, is one of the easiest ways for the therapist to observe the repetitive patterns, to step back and view the whole family as the unit of treatment. The therapist can encourage the family members to talk with each other instead of talking only with the therapist. If necessary, get up and move to another part of the room, or at least push your chair out of the circle ("I'll get out of your way while you decide that together"). Listen, observe, and comment on the family's process, and help members stay on an important issue. Question, clarify, challenge, and suggest alternatives. During all this, support the family's efforts and point out the things the members do well together.

This systemic approach concentrates on the family-as-interacting-unit by focusing directly on the family relationships (To parents: "Decide together now what you will do if your daughter uses alcohol or other drugs again."). It prevents the therapist from being caught in the middle, wedged into the restrictive roles of advocate, arbiter, judge and jury, especially when a family member asks the therapist, "Isn't there something *you* can do to keep him (or her) from drinking again?" Becoming less central in the session allows the therapist to step back and more clearly see the patterns and sequences that work against the family's recovery (e.g., the more one member sets limits on the person's chemical use, the more another member becomes lenient and protective). Finally, and just as important, when the therapist is less in the center of conversations, he or she has less chance of being inducted by the family.

TRAP 2: *Getting Bogged Down in Induction*

Induction means being pulled into the family's emotional network. Inducted therapists have lost objectivity and a balanced view of the situation. In its extreme form, it's like being in one's own family, in which objectivity is impossible.

Some hints that induction is happening are when the therapist:
— blames one member for the family problems
— feels intimidated by one or more members
— gives frequent "lectures" and good advice
— feels reluctant to challenge, or move, or create enactments, or segment, or do anything therapeutically active
— argues with a family member
— follows the family's random, disorganized agenda rather than pursuing a therapeutic direction

Induction demonstrates a family's power to eliminate an outside threat simply by making it a part of the family system. Induction occurs when the therapist gets too involved. The therapist finds himself or herself trying to "fix the family" or feeling betrayed, disappointed, or even angry when the family doesn't respond in the right ways.

Although there are many forms of induction, its commonest form in CD family therapy is when the therapist inadvertently takes sides against the CD member. For example, during a marital session I supervised, the female therapist helped the wife educate the husband about the effects of his alcohol use on the family. This conversation quickly became a two-on-one situation with predictable results. The husband reacted to the therapist the same way he had responded to his wife—resistant, detached, and defensive. After the interview the therapist commented, "Boy, is he tough!"

This unintentional side-taking happens frequently, and when it does, the therapist will eventually feel as powerless as the other family members. The therapist in this example must find a way to avoid taking on the wife's battle for her, "helping" her convince her husband of the errors in his thinking. One way for the therapist to do this is to provide a contrast to the wife in how she talks to her spouse. If the wife is highly verbal, the therapist can be brief in her remarks; if the wife is withdrawn, the therapist should be more talkative; if the wife attacks him, the therapist needs to find a way to positively reframe his behavior, and hers.

Another way to avoid induction is for the therapist to maintain more focus on the reciprocal *relationship* between the spouses (To both members: "I notice that when you (wife) offer information to your husband about his drinking, he becomes annoyed, which makes you try harder."). These moves help both to avoid a coalition between the therapist and the non-using family member and to prevent the therapist from becoming—in the CD member's eyes—just another nagging spouse.

Most therapists can spot induction quickly when it's happening to a colleague, but when it's happening to them it's not as simple to recognize. Therapists may even deny that they're powerless with the family because they're too involved. This is a professional form of denial and is almost exactly the same process as the family members' denial of what they are doing with each other.

I was completely oblivious to my first experience of being inducted. A blended family of five with a chemically dependent son habitually laughed and made jokes during the session, mostly instigated by a jovial father. Other family members and I would laugh with him. My trainer, who observed behind a one-way mirror, let this continue for the first interview to allow me to join with the family, but prior to the second session she suggested a new goal—to get the family to take the problem seriously. "Use the word 'serious' at least four times during the session," she advised me. "If family members laugh, don't laugh with them." My trainer wanted me to realize that the family had captured me, organized my behavior, and made me a part of its inappropriate reaction to a life-threatening problem.

Induction is not always negative. Neither is it always avoidable. Some degree of emotional involvement and loss of objectivity is a normal part of doing therapy with families. In the first and possibly second family session, the therapist lets himself or herself be partially pulled in by the family emotions. This is part of the joining work during the initial sessions, and it allows the therapist to understand how the family feels. Emotional engagement with the family also makes the therapist's work personally rewarding and meaningful.

The therapist must be aware, however, that his or her personal needs, values, and biases may get in the way of what the family needs. The therapist needs to ask: "Am I angry at this alcoholic parent because of my unresolved anger at my alcoholic parent?" "Does the behavior of this adolescent remind me of my own teenager?" "Does this intimidating father make me feel powerless?" "Am I taking too much responsibility for this family because of *my* need for them to get better?"

To avoid getting hooked by one person in a family (in my example, the jovial father) or by a particular family issue, the therapist must keep the *family members'* relationships as the focus, not the *therapist's* relationship with each member. With experience, therapists' ability to monitor their own level of induction improves. A trusted colleague, with whom we can discuss our cases or who joins us in a session or who watches our video taped sessions can be a major protection against our getting and/or remaining inducted into a family.

TRAP 3: *Switching the Problem Person*

The chemically dependent person is the gateway to the family. Therapists enter through that gate or they don't get in. The CD member offers the only reason therapists have to be inquiring into a family's business. If therapists try to go through another gate they will be considered trespassers and won't be tolerated long. Consider the example below.

A mother, father, sixteen-year-old son, and fourteen-year-old daughter come to family therapy because of the son's alcohol use and his trouble at school, at home, and with the law. During the initial interview the son blurts out, "I don't know why everybody is jumping on me. Dad gets drunk more than I do!" The father reacts quickly, "That's not true. Besides, I can handle it. My drinking never got us in the kind of trouble you're in." As the father and son argue, the mother and daughter say nothing. If you were the therapist, what would you do?

Some therapists think that you should deal with the father's drinking because neither the son nor the family can get better until the father's alcohol use stops. Also, if you help the family avoid the topic of the father's drinking, you become a professional enabler. Both are good reasons to include the father's drinking as a presenting problem.

And yet, a practical little voice should be whispering in your ear: "Careful here. Don't switch the problem person. If the focus switches to the father's drinking too soon, he may drop out and take the family with him. Be patient, and keep the family in therapy together."

Keep the focus on the son (and his alcohol use) at least during the first three or four sessions. Why? For three reasons: (1) The teenager needs attention first because he is usually more vulnerable to the effects of chemical use (safety, legal, school problems); (2) Focusing on the son's welfare provides the parents with a *common goal*, thereby giving the therapist access to the all-important parental relationship; (3) The family shows by its attendance that it will accept the son as having the identified problem; the family members have not shown their willingness to accept the father's chemical dependence as the identified problem.

To keep the therapy on track, the therapist should address the son: "Well, your father is above legal drinking age, and even though drinking may not be good for him, he's mature enough to make his own decision. For now, your parents are worried about you." To the parents the therapist can comment, "Once your son gets better, you are free to bring up other issues in your family. Let's deal with one problem at a time."

What about the professional enabling? Temporarily at least, the therapist is enabling by taking this approach. But if the family leaves treatment, it could return to several more months or years of untreated chemical dependence.

Why not tackle both problems at once, the son's and the father's chemical dependence? Doing this would create a hot potato to be tossed back and forth, and therapy is not likely to be effective. When the son's problem becomes too heated, he will be able to shift the focus back to his father. This bouncing around creates confusion, conflict, and frustration and is not likely to be tolerated by the father for long. It's a poor beginning for therapy and is likely to have a poor ending.

Switching the focus to the chemical use of a parent, even though it's highly relevant to the family's problems, is not recommended. When the presenting problem is a child, the therapist's premature attention to a parent's chemical use can often lead to unsuccessful treatment of the chemically dependent child and the family.

TRAP 4: *Flying Solo*

Counselors or therapists who work entirely alone with families go home talking to themselves. They are trying to make sense of what happened in a family session, which is not always clear. Most family communication is subtle and nonverbal, a dimly lit room of shifting shadows, where emotions and impressions replace facts and logic. If things get strange, support from colleagues really helps.

A CD counselor can use colleague support in several ways:

— Getting clinical supervision for your family therapy
— Talking to another CD counselor about a family you are seeing or a session you just had
— Asking a colleague to join you in the family session to get a first-hand sample
— Using a one-way mirror or video recorder to allow a colleague to view your work with the family
— Mapping the family on the blackboard while you explain who is close and who is distant, who is the powerful doorkeeper in the family, and who is the doormat.

Sharing and conversing with team members protects therapists from becoming lost and confused by their own subjective reactions to the family. Therapists who work with CD families need support, feedback, sharing, and someone to talk with when the going gets difficult or confusing. Working alone can lead to a loss of objectivity and burnout, while working with colleagues is uplifting and provides greater learning for the therapist.

Working As a Team

Here are seven types of colleague teamwork that I have used effectively in family therapy for chemical dependence.

1. Colleague Consult

One therapist works with the family alone but talks to the colleague before and after each session. By describing the family and its process, therapists can increase their objectivity and clarify their thinking. It works better if colleagues do this for each other, both serving as consultant to each other's cases.

2. Temporary Co-Therapist

With the parents' permission, ask a colleague to join you for one session with the family. Introduce the colleague and explain to the family: "We sometimes work together to get a second opinion of how we can be the most help to your family." Plan beforehand how the two of you will work together—how active each will be, who will lead the session, and the therapeutic plan to follow.

3. Reflecting Colleague

At any point during a family session, a colleague is brought in and introduced to the family: "The way we sometimes work is to use two heads instead of one. To get another viewpoint, I have asked Jane to sit with us a while. She will sit apart from us and not be part of the conversation. Occasionally, she and I may talk together while you listen."

Two or three times during the session the therapist and colleague talk to each other in front of the family. The colleague reflects to the therapist what she sees, hears, thinks, and feels about the family. Anything is permissible, as long as it shows respect for the family and its situation. Families show great interest in these conversations, which can add a new dimension to the thinking of both the family and the therapist.

4. **Expert Colleague**

For the strategic purpose of gaining power and influence, the therapist may need to call on an "expert." For example, introduce the colleague as one "who is experienced at talking with children about this problem." With the parent's permission, the child goes to another room with the colleague for an assessment interview. This segmenting allows both the IP and the other family members to speak more freely and to add new information. The assessment can be discussed with the parents at the next session, with or without the colleague's presence.

5. **Student Colleague**

Introduce the colleague as one who is "learning to work with families and whose observations and questions may be valuable to the family." During the session the student colleague asks the therapist deliberately naive questions. Examples:

— "The mother seems willing to try that, but do you think the father is willing?"
— "What will happen if the mother treats the son one way and the father treats him another?"
— "How will the parents' plan with the son affect the two other children?"

The therapist answers the questions and talks with the colleague while the family listens.

6. **Mirror Observation**

One or more colleagues observe part or all of a session from behind a one-way mirror. The family is told that they are being observed: "We often work as a team. My colleagues are behind that mirror, and I may leave briefly to talk with them. We have found this to be the most effective way to help families."

Here are several ways to use the mirror:
— The therapist leaves during the session to talk to the colleague(s) behind the mirror.
— The colleague comes into the room for a conversation with the therapist in front of the family.
— The colleague calls the therapist into the room over a phone installed for that purpose (or regular telephone) to make a suggestion or observation.
— Colleagues enter the room and "reflect" with each other or with the therapist (as in Reflecting Colleague above).
— All these can happen at different times during one or more sessions.

7. Videotape

A video recording can be made of a session, introduced to the family by: "We frequently work as a team in helping families, which includes videotaping. We are being taped now. Later, my colleague and I will review the tape to be sure we haven't missed anything important. After the tape is used for this purpose it is erased, usually within a week. Here is a form for you to sign, which gives us permission for the taping."

Very often, much can be observed on videotape that was overlooked in the family session. The videotape also directly informs colleagues about the family, allowing the colleague to be more useful in making observations and suggestions. If video is not available, use an audio recorder.

Pointers for Working With Colleagues

1. Colleague teamwork is different from supervision. Colleague work implies a peer relationship between co-workers. The therapist in charge of the case makes the final decision about how to use the suggestions.

2. Decide in advance how you will work together. Can the mirror observing colleague phone in? Come into the room? What is the role of the temporary co-therapist? What is the strategic purpose in using the colleague "expert"?

3. Don't get too long-winded with colleagues outside the room while the family waits. About 4-5 minutes is long enough for the therapist to be absent from the family. Focus on what to do during this session, and wait until after the session to discuss all the interesting personalities and the process in the family. When you return to the room, it is usually not necessary to tell the family the contents of your talk with the colleague.

4. If several colleagues are behind the mirror, they should decide on *one person* to talk with the therapist when he or she consults with the team. The therapist can be overwhelmed by too many well-meaning colleagues bursting with advice.

5. Set aside time after the session to talk with your colleagues about the session and what to do next session.

The Systemic Communication Style

Probably the best way for the therapist to minimize the risk of falling into the four traps outlined above is learning to communicate a systemic, interactional view of family relationships. A systemic style of communication refers to the therapist's ability to use his or her mannerisms, communication and social skills, inflection, tone of voice, and perceptual abilities, to convey to families the idea of the interdependence of their behavior as a family unit. That style is the degree to which therapists are able to use their whole range of expression to convey the whole-family-message discussed in Chapter 2.

Asking Questions

Sometimes therapists ask questions to obtain important factual information. At other times, therapists use questions to make an
important statement. For example, asking "What happened when you
and your husband tried to reach a decision together about how to
respond to your son?" not only serves as a search for the facts, but also
as a way of making a statement of fact, namely, "It's good for you and
your husband to talk together about this."

Therapists can also use questions to explore their own confusion
during a session. Often, such questions stir up good information. "Let
me try to understand this. You both have your ways of helping your
daughter, but sometimes these ways are different. Could she be
confused about what you expect?" Or, "I'm puzzled; last week you
were in close agreement about what plan to follow with your daughter.
Can you help me understand why the plan failed?"

Punctuating Interactions

Because interactions between people are circular—each response
creating a different reaction, which, in turn, prompts a different
response—it doesn't matter at which part of the circle the therapist
enters, or punctuates. Thus, when a wife is passively reacting to her
husband's aggression, the therapist can intervene in the sequence by
making a comment to either spouse. To the wife: "I notice that when
your husband becomes intense about this topic, you back off and give
him more space." To the husband: "Your wife's silence makes you
believe she agrees with what you say." Either way, the therapist is
trying to bring attention to a repetitive sequence that might block
change.

Sometimes an interaction between family members can be punctuated by directing remarks to the speaker, but commenting to the receiver, or even the listeners, is often more powerful. When the mother angrily says to the father, "You're not home enough to see what goes on!" the therapist could ask the father, "Did you hear what I heard—that your wife, in her own way, is asking for your support?" Or, to their son or daughter, "What do you suppose your mom really means when she says that to your dad?"

Emphasizing Behavior

Instead of, "How did you *feel* when that happened?" the therapist can ask, "What did you *do* when that happened?" Family members establish their patterns with each other according to one another's observable behavior, not according to each other's feelings, which can only be inferred.

Rather than verbally exploring a member's feelings and thoughts, the therapist can help to create the actual behavior by saying, "*Turn* to him and tell him about that." Rather than hearing about separate plans from the parents about how to deal with a drug-using teenager, more parental teamwork is prompted by saying, "Decide together now what you will do if he or she does that again."

Instead of the verb "feel," therapists can use the verb "react." This word permits a more flexible response. "How did you *react* when . . . ?" allows the client to respond not only with a feeling, but also with a thought, or with a behavior, or with all three. To family members who resist expressing feelings, this is sometimes a less threatening question than "How did you *feel* . . . ?"

Giving Credit and Responsibility

Some family therapists use the pronoun "we" when speaking to families. Using "you," however, helps therapists give credit where credit is due. "*You* did some nice work together on reaching that agreement" (not, "*we* did . . ."); or "I will help *you* work out *your* plan together if that happens again." Using "you" gives the family the responsibility for its actions: "When *you* made that decision it was scary, but *you* were able to make it stick" or "If *you* can stand together as parents, your daughter will be less confused about *your* intentions."

The family members do the hard work of change—they take the risks, they have the final responsibility, and they get the credit.

Matching the Family Mood

Matching the family mood (depressed, happy, cautious, active, concerned, etc.) is important during the initial session, and also for a few minutes at the beginning of each session. As the session progresses, however, the therapist may want to present a different mood to offer other possibilities. If family members are using inappropriate laughter to hide their anxiety, therapists can become more serious in their affect and tone of voice. If family members are silent and inactive, therapists can slowly become more active and animated. If families show a lot of nervous energy, therapists can offer calm energy.

It's a matter of being sensitive to the flow of feelings in the session. When the air is heavy with painful emotion, it's time to slow down and feel compassion and empathy with the family's struggle, to just be with the people in the moment. It's not the time for therapists to charge ahead with their own agenda.

Giving Explanations

Too much explanation can kill discovery. If the therapist sets up an enactment between members that becomes intense and meaningful to them and then interrupts to "illuminate" or explain a certain point, he or she has interfered, not facilitated. The interaction would have been better without the therapist's explanations and insights. At tense moments family members may let the therapist intrude because it's a distraction from their uncomfortable (but important) feelings. Therapists should try to remember that they are guides rather than teachers.

In their attempts to share with a family the understanding they have, therapists sometimes talk too much. Therapists need to remember three things: (1) What the family says is usually (but not always) more important than what therapists say; (2) Therapists must try to reduce the quantity and volume of their message in order to hear the family's message; (3) If therapists usually do most of the talking, they're working too hard and taking too much responsibility.

Using Family Metaphors

One father used metaphors and humor when talking about trying to get his son to work hard, to take a direction in his life, to overcome his laziness: "If he got paid for lying down, he'd get up and quit. He ain't got his cap on straight." The therapist can join with this man by using some of his metaphors: "So you and your wife would like to help him learn how to wear his cap with more pride?"

To direct a co-dependent who is taking too much responsibility for the spouse's recovery, the therapist might say, "He has a disease but you're not a nurse." To parents, when emphasizing the importance of their children attending sessions, the therapist can remark, "Your children are the heartbeat of your family; they help keep it alive." To a member who just made a statement about another's chemical use being the rest of the family's problem, not his, the therapist could quip, "Are you saying there's a bad leak in *their* end of the boat?"

Creating Intensity

The therapist can highlight important subjects to create intensity in the session. Using enactments (see Chapter 4) can generate emphasis and block distracting side-trips by putting the spotlight on an interaction between and among family members and leaving it there long enough to generate some heat.

Segmenting (see Chapter 4) also adds intensity. If a therapist wants to emphasize something to the parents, and if it seems appropriate, he or she can ask the parents if the children can wait outside. This not only narrows the field of concentration for both therapist and family, it also adds importance to the topic.

Repetition creates intensity and is often needed to exceed the high threshold of deafness we all seem to have when we don't understand something or we don't want to hear it. Important messages from family members or from the therapist need repetition, preferably with different words and with proper timing.

Keeping It Simple and Brief

Make a clear statement, and keep it brief and simple. Therapists should be alert for jargon in their language. We too often forget that families aren't familiar with our therapeutic or systemic terminology.

Short sentences are better than long ones, and the best filling between sentences is a reasonable silence. Family members need time to understand and to find words for their feelings and thoughts, to consider, ponder, or just try to absorb what is happening. They need the therapist's pauses.

Using Proper Pacing

Frequently, therapists may want positive change to happen more quickly than they have a right to expect. Sometimes we can be too eager, active, pushy, or directive. Therapists need to realize that change in behavior can begin quickly, but doesn't usually develop quickly. Something new takes getting used to. It's like shopping for clothes—several garments are tried on until one fits and becomes part of the wardrobe.

Therapists can get so wrapped up in their own therapeutic agenda that they become insensitive to the family's agenda. That's why therapists need to pace themselves, take the time to listen to the family's message, and adequately understand its concerns. Discovering a therapeutic direction to take is one thing; knowing how fast to pursue it is quite another. Hearing the same story many times can convince therapists that they know the situation well enough to step up the pace of therapy, but when their tempo is too fast, it's easy to miss some of the critical cues from the family along the way. Therapists can learn to take periodic breaks from their therapeutic direction, let it lie still for a while, then get back to it later.

~~~~~~~~~~~~~

At one time or another, therapists will be caught in all four traps. Traps are part of conducting family therapy for CD problems. But the systemic process of thinking and communicating can help to avoid many of the pitfalls inherent in such work. With chemically dependent families, traps and therapeutic mistakes are inevitable. Families are too complex for therapists to expect otherwise. As therapists, our biggest failure is not in getting trapped or in making mistakes, but in failing to learn from them, thereby making the same mistake over and over. An honest evaluation, with the help of colleagues, of what we could do differently to produce a different outcome, can make the experience of falling into a trap a permanent part of our learning. In the process, we become less afraid of confusing territory because we have emerged from swamps before.

Part Three

Guidelines for Practicing the Family Systems Approach

Chapter 7

Getting Families in for Therapy

The most important step in family therapy for chemical dependence is the first one—getting families in. When recruitment goes well, family therapy fulfills its promise of adding excitement and effectiveness to a treatment program.

Because of the routine nature of intakes in many CD treatment centers, we can easily underestimate the impact of the first family session on a family. The first session is anything but routine in the family's eyes. Guilt, anger, denial, shame, and fragile hope accompany most families to the first session. The family may also be embarrassed by admitting—just by coming to treatment—that the chemical dependence is a family issue instead of an individual one. Some family members believe that the therapist will blame them for the problem. And finally, family members are tired. They want a vacation from the topic, especially after their failures and frustrations at trying to talk about the problem with the CD family member.

In spite of these resistant feelings, most family members will attend family sessions. Some are grateful that the therapist recognizes the effects of the problem on everyone in the family and is willing to hear their side of the story. Others attend because of a sincere desire to do whatever they can to help the CD family member recover from his or her chemical dependence. Parents will often attend family sessions because of their concern over the emotional and behavioral disturbances of the children or the general tension and conflict in the home.

Whom to Recruit

Who decides who will attend the first family session? If a family member decides, the therapist may be playing into some of the family splits and conflicts that are part of the CD problem. Therapy goes better when the therapist decides who will attend.

Initially, invite everyone living in the home of the CD client, including all children, regardless of age. This applies whether the CD client is a parent or a child. By inviting everyone, the therapist is making the important therapeutic statement that the whole family is affected by the disease of chemical dependence.

Practically speaking, however, the therapist may settle for less than everyone in the home for the first interview. In families with children below age eight, the therapist may want to see only the parents and the older children for the first interview. Young children can be distracting during an assessment session and make the information gathering more difficult. In an intact family, the most important members to get to attend the first interview are the spouse of the CD client, or both parents if the CD client is a young person living at home. The missing members can be invited to the second or a later session.

If the chemically dependent person is a child living in a two-parent household, it is important to get *both* parents to come to therapy. If the CD client is a minor, one way to obtain parent cooperation is for the parents to sign a document giving the treatment center permission to treat their child. Include in the document a statement such as, "By signing below, both parents or legal guardians are consenting to attend sessions for the CD client's treatment when requested by the profes-sional staff."

Unfortunately, although many adolescent programs say that they treat families, they actually settle for involving only one of the parents in a two-parent household. Too often, siblings are also omitted from these "family" sessions with the adolescent. This results in working with only the most involved parent and the child, which can make successful therapy difficult.

In a two-parent family, seeing only one parent with the adolescent CD client inadvertently supports one of the common problems in CD families: one parent is too involved with the CD teenager and the other is too distant. The parent-child overinvolvement can contribute to family disharmony and disagreements and even contribute to supporting or maintaining the chemical use of the adolescent. The enabling by the enmeshed parent and the conflict between the mother and father about how to handle the problem prevents any unified limit-setting on the child's alcohol or other drug use. To the degree one parent is placating, close, and lenient, the other is angry, detached, and strict. This unhealthy split is being supported, even reinforced, if only the overinvolved parent is allowed to attend with his or her adolescent. Figure 7.1 is typical of such family patterns.

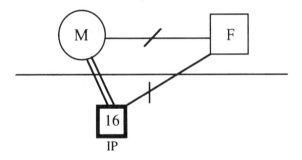

Figure 7.1. Family Pattern Before Treatment

Figure 7.1 shows a close mother-son relationship, with the father-son and the mother-father in conflict. If only the mother and son are recruited for family sessions, we may be moving the family toward the pattern in Figure 7.2.

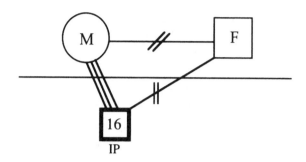

Figure 7.2. Family Pattern After Treatment

This new pattern indicates an even closer relationship (actually, enmeshment) between mother and son and a more conflictual relationship between mother-father and father-son. Mother and son are made closer because they are bonded together in the relatively intimate context of therapy, while excluding the father and other family members. The mother-father relationship is made more conflictual and distant for the same reason. This encourages divided parenting.

An additional problem can arise with this arrangement. The father will often attempt to undermine any changes brought about by therapy, largely because he disagrees with the plan created by the mother, son, and therapist. Or he may become uncooperative and apathetic around the whole issue, allowing the mother to handle it, abdicating his responsibility, and criticizing when the treatment doesn't seem to help. If the parents already have disagreements on how to respond to the problem child, refusing to be involved could be the father's way of saying that the mother is wrong in the way she parents their child.

Faced with the choice of seeing a CD adolescent and only one parent from a two-parent household, or of leaving the child out of the initial interview and seeing *both* parents, take the parents. This may seem strange—leaving out the CD client—but it is possible to conduct effective family therapy for the chemical dependence of a young person living at home without the young person initially coming to treatment. In fact, in cases in which a chemically dependent young person refuses to seek separate treatment by entering a treatment program, getting both parents into family treatment can be the first step in providing the incentive for the young CD client to enter treatment for himself or herself.

The usual therapeutic direction in such cases is to help the parents, as heads of the family, to negotiate their limits, that is, how much they are willing to tolerate from their CD child before they use their power and emotional influence to get the young person into treatment. Or, if the client is eighteen or older, the initial therapeutic goal is to prepare the parents to give their child this ultimatum: "We love you and we want to help. But if you continue to use alcohol or other drugs while living here, you must either go to treatment or leave home." The highest priority, as in all family therapy for chemical dependence, is for the CD member to enter his or her own separate treatment for the disease.

For a blended family with an adolescent CD client, the following type of case is common: A remarried mother has custody of her adolescent son, who also has regular visits to the household of his remarried father. The mother calls for an appointment for the son, who is in trouble with chemicals. Whom do you invite to the initial interview? In this case I prefer to invite everyone living in the home of the adolescent: the mother, stepfather, and siblings or step-siblings. Initially, the biological father and his wife need not be included in the therapy. As a general rule, ex-spouses with current spouses make a poor mix in family therapy, especially in the critical initial interview.

In the case outlined above, it is important to keep in mind during the sessions that the chemically dependent adolescent has two homes— the biological mother and stepfather in one, and biological father and stepmother in the other. The parents in one household may not know what goes on in the other. This could easily contribute to the son hiding his chemical dependence for a while or relapsing without the parents' knowledge. The home in which the CD client is primarily living is usually the primary system—the one involved on a daily basis, the one that must endure the most immediate consequences from intoxicated behavior, from breaking curfews, and from family conflicts and arguments around the problem. It's also the household that can provide the most immediate influence and help for the recovering teenager.

This does not mean, however, that the biological father is unimportant in the problem or in the solution. During the initial interview with the CD client's primary household, the therapist should inquire in detail about the amount and type of contact between the son and the biological father and his blended family in the other household. If the contact is significant, it should be considered a coparenting arrangement, which requires a separate session with the mother, son, and biological father. This procedure also applies to separated or divorced single parents, when both parents have regular contact with the adolescent CD client.

One or more of these separate sessions with the two biological parents and child may be needed. The purpose of such meetings should be clarified at the outset: "We are here to discover how the two of you can help your son recover from chemical dependence." Make clear that the session is not an attempt to resolve any of the ex-spouses' leftover marital anger and conflict, if any remain. The focus is on their coparenting agreements, and how they may influence their CD adolescent's recovery. Avoid rehashing marital history.

Working with the biological parents alone, without the son's presence, may be necessary to help the parents work through their disagreements about their son. Once the parents reach agreements on visitation schedules, rules for the son's behavior, and other coparenting issues, bring in the son and let the parents tell him their decisions. Also, each biological parent is responsible for telling his or her respective spouse, children, and stepchildren about the content of the joint session(s) and the agreements made between the biological parents concerning the CD son.

In summary, recruiting CD families for therapy begins with the decision about whom to invite. The general rule is to invite everyone living in the household of the CD client, plus any other person who has been mentioned by the caller (with the exception for blended families noted above) as being involved in the problem situation. Get as many people to the initial interview as possible. It is always easier later to reduce the number attending than to increase it.

How to Recruit

When families are afraid that family therapy will expose all their hurt, shame, and anger, what will encourage them to attend an initial interview? Aside from legal leverage, there seems to be three main motivations: (1) family members want their CD member to stop using alcohol or other drugs and to receive some help; (2) someone in the family insists that the whole family attend; and (3) the outpatient or inpatient treatment program to which the CD individual is referred persuades them to get help for the whole family.

These motivations provide suggestions to the therapist on how to get the family to the first interview:

1. Emphasize the need for information from the family to help the CD member recover.
2. Keep the parent(s) in charge of recruiting the family. Encourage them to use their influence to get their children to attend.
3. State the treatment agency's policy about family attendance. To the CD client say, "The way we work is to see everyone living in the home so they will understand their part in helping. You don't have to do all the changing in the family." To a CD client's spouse say, "Our policy is to have a meeting with your family to see how we can all do our part to help Bob stay sober" or "Our policy is to meet with everyone in the home who knows about the problem."
4. Make whole-family statements: "To make this treatment effective, we need to hear the concerns of everyone in your family who is affected by the alcohol or other drug use."

If the therapist follows the four guidelines listed and discussed below, the chances of recruiting families will be improved.

1. View recruitment as an agency-wide issue.
2. Involve the family early in the process.
3. Don't depend entirely on the CD client to recruit the family.
4. Leverage: Use it if you need it.

View Recruitment as an Agency-wide Issue

Family recruitment should be a total agency commitment, not an isolated contest between the therapist's techniques and the family's resistance. Successful recruitment involves the agency administration, its office staff, and the record-keeping procedures.

Administration's commitment to family therapy will ultimately determine the amount of success in family attendance. The agency's executive director and supervisors control its important resources—space, time, policies and money. A different meeting space may be needed because many therapists' offices are not large enough to accommodate a family. The agency's and staff's working hours may need to include evening appointments. The agency's treatment policies will determine the amount of firmness and leverage therapists can use in getting families in. And when required, time and money are needed for training and supervision.

The receptionists and front office staff who make initial appointments are also part of the effort. In fact, they are a vital—and frequently overlooked—resource in a treatment program. If they do not understand the rationale for working with the family for CD problems, they are not likely to make an effective attempt to convince the family member who calls to bring everyone in the home for the initial interview. Give the agency's receptionist staff its rightful place on the treatment team. Include these staff members in case conferences, clinical meetings, and training workshops, and invite them to view videotaped therapy sessions. These important people are in the front lines of the agency's service. Once they are encouraged to participate, they are usually interested and eager to learn the reasons for therapy with families and to spread the news to the families they encounter in the initial contacts.

The records policies and charting procedures are another important aspect of the treatment system. Many treatment centers, especially those in the public sector, require additional documentation to conduct family therapy, such as opening a new chart on each family member who attends sessions. This extra paperwork tends to discourage counselors from recruiting families for therapy. Someday record-keeping procedures may catch up to the clinical methods. In the meantime, an expedient solution is to keep an individual chart for the CD client and to include the family members as additional contacts in his or her treatment.

Treatment programs vary widely on the importance they give to including the family in treatment. At one end of the spectrum, some inpatient and, less often, outpatient programs will refuse any treatment unless the family is involved. At the other extreme are programs that treat the individual with no family contact at all, even phone contact.

Since an effective family program for CD treatment depends on success in recruiting families, and since recruitment depends on agency-wide administrative support, therapists may want to use some of the ideas listed below when talking to agency administrators about increasing the use of family therapy as a treatment approach. Remember, when administration is convinced that it wants a viable family program, there will be one.

1. Most programs recognize that CD is a family illness. Over 90% of CD treatment programs offer some kind of services to families. (From a random selection of 110 treatment programs in the 1988-89 Treatment Directory published by the U.S. Journal of Alcohol and Drug Dependence, 100 programs listed "Family Services" as part of their services.)

2. When the family is involved, treatment is briefer. Five to seven sessions is the average. For comparison with this number, the therapist could calculate the average number of individual sessions per CD client in his or her caseload. (My experience shows that family therapy is 25-40% briefer than individual therapy; this means more clients served per year but not necessarily more clients on the rolls at any given time.)

3. In family treatment, more people receive treatment at the same expenditure of staff time. A session with a family of six takes no more time than an individual session.

4. Because it's shorter treatment and higher turnover, the agency cost per patient is lower.

5. Family therapy has prevention benefits. For example, if a family with a CD adolescent can make progress in therapy, problems that may develop later in younger siblings will be handled more effectively by the parents with the new skills the parents have learned in family therapy.

6. Since family therapy is more of a team effort than individual therapy, it can have beneficial effects on staff peer support, sharing, and learning together.

Involve the Family Early in the Process

Treatment centers that successfully recruit families have found that the earlier in the treatment process families are urged to attend, the greater the chances that they will do so. Therefore, family recruitment should start at the very beginning. When someone calls for an individual appointment, ask the caller the names and ages of everyone living in the home. After hearing the caller's view of the problem, and toward the end of the conversation, invite everyone by name to the intake interview. For example, "I would like to have you and Jeff (husband) and your children, Sandra, Ted, and Robin for the first meeting. Our policy is to see everyone in the home to get a complete picture of your situation."

If the caller is the CD client and adamantly refuses to bring the family, ask him or her to come alone. From a clinical standpoint, however, remember that the longer a CD client is in individual treatment without the family, the less likely it becomes that the family will attend. Family members are frequently reluctant to come and talk with the CD client's individual counselor, partly because they believe the counselor is biased toward the client's view of the situation.

In other cases, the initial caller may acknowledge the need for a spouse to be present but refuse to include the children. In such a case, accommodate the client and allow all children to be omitted from the initial interview. Some parents just want to check out the environment, the counselor, and the treatment procedures before bringing their children. After the initial interview, parents may be more willing to include their children.

Don't Depend Entirely on the CD Client to Recruit the Family

When I used to put the responsibility on the CD client for getting the family in, I often ended up with no family attendance and with loads of excuses from CD clients for their family's absence. Gradually I learned to give CD clients only one chance to invite their families. If this failed, I made direct phone contact with the family members myself.

There are two reasons why this direct contact is so often needed. First, even though the CD clients may agree to get their family members to the next interview, they may not actually invite them because they really don't want them to attend. Rather than deal with all the feelings of guilt and anger toward a spouse, for example, the CD client may find it easier to say, "My (wife, husband) couldn't change his or her work schedule this week." Second, by requesting CD clients to recruit their families, the therapist may unintentionally put CD clients in an awkward position. If, for example, a CD client's spouse and children don't agree to attend, the CD client is caught between the therapist and the family—the therapist is pushing from one end, and the family is saying no from the other. This squeeze can embarrass and anger the CD client. Direct contact between therapist and family members is best.

Leverage: Use It If You Need It

Don't be afraid to use available leverage (legal, Department of Social Services, etc.) if it's needed to get the family to attend. Use any ethical means necessary to begin family treatment. Wanting to save lives and do whatever is possible to prevent severe emotional or physical harm from chemical dependence is a justifiable position, and one need not be timid or apologetic about it.

Leverage, however, doesn't have to come from the outside. It can also be generated by the policies of the treatment program itself. One such policy in inpatient treatment is that of discharging the CD client if the family refuses to attend sessions once the CD client is admitted to the treatment unit. Of course, such a policy would be explained to the CD client and family in advance of admission and in writing. An inpatient unit where I once worked had a policy of discharging the CD client if the family missed the second family appointment. The policy's leverage was very effective. Over a period of two years, the unit was forced to discharge, with appropriate referrals, only 2 out of 125 chemically dependent clients.

In outpatient treatment, internal leverage can be created by making a caring and firm statement to the initial caller about the agency's policy on family attendance. If the family doesn't show for the intake with the CD client, include conversation about the family in the intake interview with statements and questions similar to the following: "We have found that family members are usually aware of a person's alcohol or other drug use. Since you live with (name members), how are they involved in your alcohol or other drug use? What is their reaction? How do you and your spouse generally get along? What does he or she do when you use alcohol or take drugs? Tell me about your relationship with your mother and father. (Ask this whether the CD client lives with parents or not and whether the parents are alive or deceased.) Did either of your parents use alcohol or other drugs?" (If so, encourage clients to tell you anything they will about the parents' use. This helps to discover CD clients' beliefs about problem use— whether it's a character defect or disease, how they define chemical use problems, when treatment is required for the problem, etc. By telling you about their parents' use or even non-use, they will not only be "talking to themselves" about their own use of chemicals, but also connecting and comparing their use with that of one or both of their parents.) A comment by the therapist that chemical dependence often runs in families might be valuable at this point.

If an agency stands firm and persistent on its policy of family attendance, the CD clients, their families, and the referral sources in the community will eventually support it.

Recruiting Missing Members

If the treatment center emphasizes family involvement, someone from the family will often accompany the CD client to the intake session. This session is generally a standard four-part interview (see Chapter 8) with (1) the whole family, (2) the CD client only, (3) the family only, (4) the whole family.

The therapist's first priority in the session is to make those who do attend feel welcome and valuable and to communicate understanding of their situation and their anxiety, anger, and fear. The therapist also has a second priority: to discover who is missing, which may not be as easy as it sounds. Frequently, important missing member(s) do not live in the home and are not mentioned by the family member who made the initial contact or by the CD client during the intake interview. They may remain unknown to the counselor simply because they were not asked about, or the CD client and family members did not mention them because of conflict between one or more family members and the missing member.

I once had four sessions with the family of a twenty-one-year-old CD client who lived with her parents before discovering that the maternal grandmother, who lived on the same block, was not only the prime enabler, but was also the third parent in a highly conflictual parental triangle. The parents were reluctant to bring up the emotionally charged grandmother issue during the sessions or to intervene in the grandmother-granddaughter relationship, possibly because the family was living rent-free in a house owned by the grandmother. I never did get the grandmother to attend, but the parents were able to support each other and stand firm on what they would tolerate from their semi-recovering daughter. After a temporary increase in the conflict between parents and grandmother and a few relapses by the daughter, she left home, bottomed out with her drug use, admitted herself to inpatient treatment, and became serious about her recovery.

It is naive to assume that all the players in the CD drama are present and accounted for in the family sessions. Thus, during the intake session ask, "Who else knows about the problem?" Had I asked this question in the twenty-one-year-old's family above, I would have inquired further about anyone they mentioned and would have more quickly discovered the grandmother's central, enabling position in the family.

Below is a set of procedures and strategies for recruiting missing members, from mild to more extreme. Try the most routine and least intrusive methods first. If these don't work, proceed to the next strategy in the sequence. If none of them works, concentrate on helping the people who do attend.

1. Invite everyone in the home to the intake session with the statement, "Our policy is to see everyone living in the home . . . "
   a. ". . . to get a clearer picture of your situation."
   b. ". . . to better understand how we can help you and your family."
   c. ". . . to find out how your family can help you stay sober or drug free after treatment."
   d. ". . . to see if there is anyone in your family who would like to join our family program."
2. Put empty chairs in the circle of family members who are present to represent missing members. ("I will put a chair here for Margaret just to remind us that she's missing.")
3. Ask questions about missing members: "What are they like?" "What are their concerns?" "What do they think about the family being here?"
4. Ask, "Who can get the missing member(s) to attend the next session?"
5. Call the missing member(s) and talk with them about attending at least one family session.
6. Invite missing members to a separate session, without the rest of their family. After one or more separate sessions, they may agree to join the family sessions.
7. Send a brief, hand-written questionnaire via the attending members to the non-attending members. On the questionnaire ask the missing members: (a) what is their major concern in the family; (b) whether they believe the alcohol or other drug use is a problem; (c) what they recommend as a solution; (d) their opinions and feelings about what is going on in the family. Invite the attending family members to bring the written information back with them to the next session. This involves the missing members indirectly and provides information to the therapist.

8. Ask the attending members to write a letter to the missing members that includes reasons for the missing ones to attend. Each person's letter can be read aloud at the next session, if the member agrees to. It could also be mailed.

9. Audio tape a session by placing a cassette recorder in an empty chair in the circle. Before recording, explain that the tape will be given to the family. At the end of the session, give the tape to one of the adult members, saying, "This is your tape. I hope you will share it with your missing (husband, daughter, mother, or other member)." Be sure to talk about family relationships and the non-attending members during the session.

~~~~~~

   Despite their best efforts, therapists will encounter family members who just won't attend a family session for their member with an alcohol or other drug problem. At first, it seems as if they really don't care. Although it looks that way, I have found that very few family members truly don't care. Some refuse to attend in order to hide their feelings of guilt, anger, and fear. Others excuse themselves because they disagree with another member about the severity of the problem or how it should be handled; they don't want to sit and talk about it because they don't want the disagreements and conflict. Other members may not attend because they're so worn out with the problem that they refuse to be inconvenienced any more. I believe that it's important for therapists to understand these hidden but realistic reasons and not to assume that a CD client's family just doesn't care.

   If all attempts fail to involve the family of the CD client and you are satisfied that you have given family recruitment a good effort, work with the individual CD client in groups and in individual therapy and connect the CD client to his or her own recovery program (AA, NA, etc.).

Chapter 8
Session One—The Initial Interview

The initial interview is a unique session in family therapy. It is usually the easiest one for the therapist and the most difficult one for the family. For the therapist, the goal is to understand the family members and their situation, not to change them. For the family, the first step in recovery—seeking help—is usually the hardest, most anxiety-producing, and the longest in coming. The first session may also be the first and only time family members have sat together for more than a few minutes and struggled to talk about the chemical dependence problem and how it has affected them. Attempts to do this at home have probably ended in someone's refusal to talk, in arguments, or in depressing silence.

Most families are anxious before this first session, largely because they don't know what to expect. Will the therapist blame me? Will he or she think we're crazy? Will the therapist understand? Will the kids hear something they shouldn't hear? Will anyone get out of control? Whose side will the therapist take?

The purpose of the first session is to put the family at ease and to establish a therapeutic contract. The initial session also lets the family members know what they can expect of treatment, emphasizes the importance of all family members, and gets the family's commitment to return. The first interview sets the work in motion.

This all-important interview needs more structure and order than do the later sessions. A family will be more comfortable if the therapist manages the first interview with direction and purpose. Gentle control of the interview also protects the family from diving in too quickly and getting stuck in old, frustrating conversations.

It's best not to stray too far from the presenting problem. Most of the discussion should be focused around the problem behavior and the family's reaction to it ("How have you reacted to the alcohol or other drug use problem?" or "What have you done to try and solve the problem?"). Helping the family see the problem differently or broadening the problem to include the whole family is valuable in therapy, but not if it is done too early. The therapist will be more successful in working with the family by initially staying with the family members' views of the problems presented for treatment.

To give the first session some organization and structure, I use a version of the five-stage procedure for the initial interview contained in *Problem Solving Therapy* by Jay Haley. I have slightly modified these stages to make them more appropriate to family therapy for chemical dependence.

Stages of the Initial Interview

Preinterview Stage

During the first contact (usually by phone), certain information is obtained and the appointment is made for the first session. The person receiving the call:

1. Gets a brief description of the caller's perception of the problem.
2. Obtains names, ages (of children), and relationships of persons living in the home.
3. Invites everyone to the first session: "The way we work is to see everyone in the home to get a clearer picture of your situation."
4. Asks the caller to invite other family members living outside the home, such as grandparents or siblings, who are also involved.

The goals of the Preinterview Stage are to establish rapport with the caller and to invite whomever the caller will bring to the first interview. Generally, the more people present in the first interview, the better.

The preinterview contact deserves a special note. If someone from the receptionist staff takes the call, he or she should be aware of its importance. Since it probably took the caller months or years to risk making this threatening and important call, the caller may feel anxious and vulnerable. Likewise, he or she could also be angry, especially if the caller is setting the appointment involuntarily because of legal, school, or employer pressure. In addition, this contact often follows a recent crisis in the family, adding to the stress the caller feels. For these reasons, therapists and administrators should view first client contacts as clinical, not administrative, procedures. Whoever takes the phone calls to set appointments should be instructed not only on proper telephone technique and etiquette, but also on the agency's clinical policies. The receiver of the call should also be prepared for the caller's resistance at being asked to bring everyone in the home to the first interview.

Social Stage

When the family arrives, the therapist greets them and invites them to choose a seat in a prearranged circle of chairs (the therapist then takes the remaining chair). The therapist individually asks each member about himself or herself in a polite, "small-talk" fashion. The therapist asks for information about school, work, hobbies, or anything else family members will say about themselves.

The therapist:

1. Begins with one of the parents or with the oldest adult in the family and proceeds from parents to oldest children to youngest child. This sequence of addressing members supports the natural hierarchy of the family unit. If both parents are present,

and if one of them made the initial contact for the appointment, the therapist begins with the *other* parent; this balances the information sharing and, in the case of a family with a CD adolescent, draws in the (presumably) less involved parent.

2. Finds out about the extended family (grandparents, aunts, uncles, etc.). Depending on the type and amount of contact with the family, these members may be asked to attend one or more future sessions.

3. Asks several general questions that support the members' strengths as a family: "What does this family enjoy doing together?" or "Tell me about something (or someone) in the family you're proud of" or other light-hearted inquiries that reveal their competence and successes as a family.

4. Discourages discussion of the problem until the Social Stage is completed with everyone.

Usually 10-15 minutes is enough time to complete the Social Stage, depending on the number of people in the interview. The purposes of this stage are to:

1. Begin the therapy in a non-threatening way, giving the family a chance to adjust to the therapist and to the setting.

2. Establish rapport between the therapist and each family member.

3. Show that everyone in the family will be considered important and given attention by the therapist.

4. Collect information about each family member and about others outside the family who may be involved.

5. Support the family's strengths and positive qualities.

Problem Definition Stage

After the social exchange, everyone is asked separately about his or her views on the situation that brought the family to therapy.

The therapist:

1. Again starts with the parents and proceeds from oldest to youngest child.
2. Keeps the questions general at first, to allow family members room to reply in any way they like. For example:
   a. "What is your major concern in your family right now?"
   b. "How can I be of help to you?"
   c. "How do you see the family situation now?"
   d. "What led to your coming here?"
3. Avoids leading questions about alcohol or other drug use in this initial inquiry. Asking a husband, for example, "How have you dealt with your wife's alcoholism?" may alienate the family because it presumes alcoholism and implies responsibility and failure by the husband or other members.
4. Listens to each person's view of the problem situation and summarizes to the speaker the therapist's understanding of what he or she said.
5. Makes no attempt to help the family see the problem differently or to offer solutions.
6. May ask questions of a person to clarify an unclear statement of the problem. The therapist does not, however, urge anyone to reveal information or feelings that he or she may not want to disclose this early.
7. Restricts extensive dialogue between the members until everyone has been given a chance to express his or her view of the problem.

Occasionally, a hitch occurs in this stage, namely, no one mentions alcohol or other drug use, even though this is the referring problem. Usually, this is easily remedied by a question or comment by the therapist: "Our agency is here to help people and families recover from alcohol or other drug use problems. Is anyone concerned about this?"

or simply, "My information says that we're meeting because someone is concerned about Fred's drinking." This introduces the topic and gives the family permission to discuss it.

Once the topic of alcohol or other drug use is opened, other questions designed to discover the family's patterns around chemical use can be asked. For example:

—"When your son (daughter, wife, husband) was under the influence last weekend, what did you do?"

—"About how often do the arguments about alcohol or other drug use happen?"

—*To a parent:* "What does your daughter usually do when she knows her brother has been using drugs?"

—*To a spouse:* "When you get home from work and find that your wife has been using alcohol, what do you usually do?"

—*To the using member:* "How do you react to your family's ideas about your chemical use?"

The Problem Definition stage clarifies the family's ideas of the problem and gives the therapist permission to explore relevant areas of the family's functioning.

Interaction Stage

During this stage, the family members are asked to talk to each other rather than to the therapist. Prior to this, family members have *described* themselves and their situation. Now the therapist *observes* how the family members interact together. This shift from describing the problem to interacting around it often occurs spontaneously, since family members usually have different views about the problem. If the family doesn't begin to interact on its own, the therapist needs to encourage two or more members to talk together about something relevant to them. For example, the therapist can say to a parent, "You seemed puzzled at what your son did last Saturday. Ask him about that to clear up your confusion." Enactments, the technique for creating these interactions, are discussed in Chapter 4.

While the family is interacting, the therapist:

1. Asks other members, when appropriate, to join the conversation between the two interacting members ("What's your view of this?"). Bringing others into the conversation reveals everyone's involvement and gives information about family relationships.
2. Observes, points out strengths, helps them stay on the subject, gives support, uses Positive Reframing (see Chapter 5), or clarifies their dialogue. These activities facilitate the therapist's joining with the family and understanding its particular situation.
3. Decentralizes his or her (the therapist's) role as communication facilitator. If necessary, the therapist shifts his or her chair back or moves to another location in the room ("I'll get out of your way so you can talk about . . . ."). If talking to each other is too uncomfortable for family members, the therapist resumes the central role until later in the interview, or, if they are extremely reluctant, waits until the next interview to arrange an interaction between and among them.

The Interaction Stage gives valuable information about family patterns: how they communicate together; who talks to whom; who is most influential; who is allied with whom. It also prepares the family for future sessions when the therapist will sometimes become less accessible to the family in order to support them doing their own work with each other.

Closing Stage

In this final stage, the therapist:

1. Summarizes the family's views of the presenting problem(s).
2. Creates motivation for the family to return, pointing out individual and family strengths, as well as the family members' concerns about the CD member and themselves. If they

179

minimize the problem, the therapist emphasizes that it could become (or already is) dangerous and life-threatening, adding brief remarks about the progression of the disease. For those families who fully recognize the problem, the therapist presents the idea that in these meetings they will find relief and hope.

3. Gives appropriate referral information (AA, NA, Al-Anon, Naranon, agency family program, etc.).

4. Asks for a three-session commitment—two more after this one—with the statement, "After the three sessions we can look at where we are." Families are more likely to cooperate if they expect that therapy will be brief.

5. Sets the appointment for the next session.

The stages of the first interview are designed to get therapy off to a good start by staying with the presenting problem, working with benevolent control and direction, appreciating the special situation and strengths of the family, and offering hope that these meetings will be worthwhile.

The first interview is not the time to make the family aware of its enabling and denial. Doing so is improper timing and can lead to unintentionally brief family therapy. In the first session the therapist does whatever is necessary to engage with the family; this makes family therapy possible. The family should leave the first interview feeling a sense of relief and thinking, "That wasn't so bad."

Several motivators or "therapeutic hooks" can be used in the first interview to increase the chances of the family returning. Depending on the family's situation and the treatment agency's policy, one or more of the following may be useful, especially if the family's commitment to therapy is weak:

1. Combine the CD client's individual assessment with the first family interview in a three-part session: (a) meet with the whole family for a few minutes (through the Problem Definition Stage); (b) during the Interaction Stage, remove the CD client for an assessment with an intake counselor while the therapist

talks with the other family members; (c) bring the CD client back to the family session for the Closing Stage of the first interview. If appropriate, the family may be told that the intake information will be considered during the week and discussed in the next session, thus motivating the family to return to learn about the assessment results. A release of information form from the CD client is obtained for this purpose.

2. During the Closing Stage of the first interview the therapist may assign a relevant and simple Task (see Chapter 4) for the following week. Explain to the family that the outcome of this assignment will be talked about in the next session.

3. If there are young children in the interview, the therapist can get the parents' permission for the children to do several Drawings (see Chapter 5) while the therapist and adults talk. The therapist can keep these drawings and offer to discuss them at the next session, with the remark, "Drawings by children often reveal how they are thinking and feeling about the family. They usually contain some surprises." Curiosity about the content of the drawings may motivate the family to return.

4. Toward the end of the first interview, tell the parents or spouse that you will share with them at the next session some of the ways other families have dealt with this problem. Appeal to their desire for information, understanding and solutions.

Regardless of the therapist's education and experience, the best posture in the first session is to be a student of *this* family, eager to learn all about it. Being an authoritative "expert" has its place, but not this early. Generally, families will not really listen to the therapist until the therapist has really listened to them.

The Initial Interview with a Partial Family

Even when the CD client has promised to bring the family to the initial interview, missing members are common. The excuses offered ("He had to work" or "She has an exam") are sometimes legitimate, but most often they are clues to the splits, alliances, and other problematic family patterns that need to be addressed in therapy with the whole family present. Here are some suggestions for the first interview with a partial family:

1. Establish a strong positive relationship with the person(s) present and in need.

2. Since the chairs have been arranged in a circle for the number of family members expected, one or more chairs will be empty. To make the presence of the missing members important, talk about them, referring to the empty chairs. What would *they* say about the problem, what are *their* opinions about the situation? This preliminary talk about the missing members makes it reasonable—at the end of the session—to ask for others to attend: "We've talked a lot about Joe and I'd like to meet him. Who can get him here?"

3. If it appears that no one in the family can get the missing member(s) in, obtain the family's permission for you to call them the following day. During this phone conversation, certain phrases are useful:

    a. "Your family (spouse, child) needs your help."

    b. "I am trying to be impartial, but it's hard to do when I have only one side of the story."

    c. "You have a special kind of influence with your (son, daughter, brother, parents, etc.)."

    d. "I would like to meet you. All I know about you is what I hear from your spouse (children, parents, etc.)."

4. If the missing members still refuse to attend with the family, ask them to see you alone, so that you can get a more well-rounded view of the situation ("I like to meet with everyone in the family who has been affected by the problem"). After one or more of these separate interviews, they may agree to attend the family sessions. Even if they don't agree, the therapist has still gained greater understanding of the situation by talking with them.

If all attempts at getting in the missing members fail, work with those who do attend. While working with an individual or portion of a family, always keep in mind the broader family and social network in which the chemical dependence problem is embedded.

Getting Families to Return for Therapy

Reasons for Early Dropouts

The nature of family therapy, as compared to individual or group therapy, makes attrition more likely. There are simply more people to convene in family therapy than in individual therapy, and unlike group therapy, if one key family member refuses to attend, everyone may refuse.

Most CD families are propelled into treatment by an immediate crisis that often quickly dissipates. Between the time the family member calls for an appointment and the first interview—generally a lapse of one to several days—the family may have reestabilized and the crisis may have subsided, even though the family may keep the appointment. After a session's talk with the therapist and assurance that they're not all going crazy, the family members have gotten some relief. It's similar to a drop in body temperature from 103 degrees to 100 degrees—the patient still has a fever, but feels much better. Such sudden relief can convince a family that no further treatment is needed. These "one session cures" can be the family's way of protecting itself from going deeper into uncomfortable issues. If the family is to return, the member who has the influence to convene the family for therapy must be convinced that these meetings will be worthwhile.

Another reason families do not return could be the family's confusion about the nature of therapy: what they are required to do, how the therapist works, and how many sessions it will take. They may not see a clear connection between the problem they are having and the way the therapist is working: "That counselor is a nice person, but I don't see how exploring our feelings will help our son with his drug problem." To engage a family in treatment, relevance is essential. The

183

therapist must address the problems the family considers important. Staying relevant to the family's concerns helps to achieve the primary goal of the first interview—to have a second interview.

~~~~~~~~

During the first interview, the therapist works with gentle control and direction. The five stages presented in this chapter permit this control, allow for the economical use of time, and provide the needed assessment information.

1. **Preinterview Stage:** Collect the basic social and problem data; identify the family members who are invited to the initial interview; set the appointment.

2. **Social Stage:** Beginning with the parents(s), establish rapport with each member with "getting-to-know-you" small talk. Complete this brief socializing with everyone before allowing anyone to discuss the presenting problem.

3. **Problem Definition Stage:** Beginning with the parent(s)—even if a parent is the CD client—define each person's view of the problem and hear his or her story. Discourage family members from talking to each other until everyone has presented his or her view of the problem.

4. **Interaction Stage:** Through creating Enactments, encourage family members to interact with each other on a topic relevant to them. If necessary, structure the conversations to avoid chaos and confusion.

5. **Closing Stage:** Briefly summarize the family's concerns, give everyone cause for hope, and set another appointment.

Chapter 9

Beyond the Initial Interview

This chapter will not give a session-by-session account of the middle and late sessions of family therapy. Anything can happen, depending on the many variables of the particular family circumstances, on the differing wants and needs of the members, or on the personality and experience of the therapist, among others. Instead, this chapter will focus on the second and third sessions, and look at four topics that are likely to be relevant throughout the remaining family sessions: (1) the fallacies families have about CD problems; (2) family issues that are predictable in early recovery; (3) issues to watch for; (4) relapse preparation.

The Second Session

Because the therapist is still working at "engaging" the family during the second session, its overriding goal is to get the family to return for a third session. Here are some typical questions the therapist might ask himself or herself during this second session:

1. Who is still missing from the session?
2. What are some of the strengths in this family? What are the members doing that's good?
3. Who is the most and the least concerned about the alcohol or other drug problem?

4. Which family member, if any, appears to be resistant and uncooperative? How can I join with that member?
5. Who is close to whom and who is distant?
6. If it's a two-parent family, do the parents present themselves as being in agreement, disagreement, or somewhere in between?
7. What kind of enabling is going on? By whom?
8. What kind of small success can I engineer for them to have during the second session?
9. During the session, can I think of an appropriate task to assign for the coming week?

One of the therapist's highest priorities is to inquire about missing members. Did everyone expected for this second session show up, including those who were determined in the initial interview to be important but who were not present then? If new members are present in the second session, spend a brief social and problem definition time with each one, making them feel welcome and important.

If the children were absent at the initial interview, some information about them was obtained then. If they are absent at the second session, find out more about them, or about anyone else—extended family, friends or professionals—who have been involved with the family. As a general rule, the therapist should try to keep a broader view than the family about who is relevant to the problem situation.

The therapist should clarify the family's major concerns by stating what he or she understood from the first session. Ask if the family wants to add anything to what was discussed then. It's best not to assume what family members are currently worried about. Clarifying their problems and concerns can be done at any time in family therapy. The point here is to keep the sessions on target and relevant to the members.

Some families will want to tell about a happening of the past week—something a child did, an argument between two or more members, or some other recent incident. Exploring these current issues provides real-life information about the family and is relevant and important to the members. If the family takes the lead in the second session, the therapist need only follow.

Significant interventions, with the purpose of changing relationships, are usually not appropriate in the second session. The therapist doesn't yet know enough about the family. Even if he or she did, not enough rapport has been established to go directly to the most resistant patterns such as entrenched enabling or hidden conflicts and coalitions in the family. It is a good time, however, to use such techniques as Drawings, Sculpting and Movement, and Circular Questions (see Chapter 5). These are assessment exercises as well as therapeutic techniques, and they can begin to change the family's view from focusing on the CD member to focusing on its interconnected relationships, thus giving the meeting a whole-family flavor. Other techniques, appropriate at any session, are also useful here: Joining, Enactments, Segmenting (see Chapter 4), Positive Reframing, and Relabeling (see Chapter 5). Also, an appropriate Task (see Chapter 4) could be assigned for the coming week and then discussed in the third session.

A special problem sometimes occurs during these early sessions, especially if an adolescent is the CD client: the parents believe that the CD problem has disappeared, that the teenager has realized his or her error and has suddenly given up alcohol or other drugs for life. Of course, this could happen—anything could happen—but a problem serious enough to get a family into treatment is not likely to go away that easily. Such a rosy outlook also undermines the family's motivation to continue family sessions: "Now that our child is well, why should we keep having these family meetings?" The therapist knows, and the family will learn, that the work is not over when the chemical use appears to stop.

In cases like the example above, the therapist can show his or her benevolent skepticism, reminding the parents that among chemically dependent teenagers who try to abstain, about two-thirds again try chemicals more than once within the first year. Without becoming a doomsday prophet, the therapist must gently persuade the family that at least three sessions are necessary to monitor the good progress the family is making and to be sure that the chemical use has stopped.

The Third Session

The third session is special. Families often have a crisis situation to report, or something novel and interesting happens during the session. By this session, the family is usually familiar with what to expect in therapy and is comfortable enough to take a risk. Also, the family is over the immediate trauma, is less guarded, and is more willing to release emotion. Whatever the reasons, the third session may begin to uncover some of the long-standing family issues.

The CD member has usually been on the "hot seat" for the first two sessions. The third session is a good time to spread the focus, to more actively involve everyone. The therapist becomes more active in mixing up the interactions—sometimes being central to the communications, sometimes setting up Enactments and getting out of the family's way. For example, when the wife says, "My husband never listens to me," the therapist may reply, "See if you can get him to listen to you now." If a parent says, "Our son hasn't used drugs, but he's withdrawn and won't communicate with us," the therapist might say, "Try to get him to talk with you now." If a parental lecture ensues, the therapist can move into New Talk (see Chapter 5). Changing the seating arrangements can be also be an indirect communication to the family about its relationships: "It's awkward for the two of you to talk together while your daughter is sitting between you. Is it okay if she moves?"

If a dangerous or crisis situation seems likely to occur, it's not too early to talk about having a Brief Network Intervention (see Chapter 5). Perhaps the only technique that would be premature in the third session is Alter Ego (see Chapter 5), and even this should not be ruled out if the therapist has developed good rapport and trust with the family.

Beyond the third session, it's not possible to predict the family's specific issues and difficulties. It is predictable, however, that the therapist will encounter resistance when family members begin to delve deeper into uncomfortable issues among them and when they begin to change the way they view the CD problem. Resistance comes in many forms, and much of it has its origin in how the family members are thinking about the problem. As we'll see in the next section, many of their notions are not realistic.

Common Fallacies Held by Families

Families often have misconceptions about chemical dependence. Some come from their lack of information about the disease, and some from their natural lack of objectivity. These fallacies give birth to much of the denial and resistance in the early stages of family therapy.

Much of the misinformation about chemical dependence can be corrected by the family orientation and education sessions, which are part of most CD programs that treat families (see Chapter 1). In spite of the lectures, films, and discussions about chemical dependence that are normally a part of the educational component of treatment, many family members will still hold on to their old ideas about the disease. If these misconceptions and fallacies arise in the therapy sessions, the therapist should respond to them.

The most common of these fallacies are listed below. They reveal how family members may be thinking. Each fallacy is accompanied by suggested responses, which, of course, should be modified by the therapist's judgment of the particular case.

Family Fallacy #1: *Family members don't need help. We don't have the problem.*

Family's view: "He (the CD member) is the only one in the family who uses alcohol or other drugs. He's the one who has hangovers and gets in trouble because of his drinking and using. It's his problem. The only help we need is for the professionals to get him sober and straight."

Professional's view: "When someone is dependent on chemicals, everyone in the family is pulled into it one way or another, sometimes by doing more than his or her share of the family work, sometimes by protecting each other from the problem, and sometimes by working hard to keep the family together. All of these cause strong emotions such as anger, fear, and hopelessness. When everyone in the family can understand and overcome these emotions, the family can get a fresh start."

Family Fallacy #2: *The one using the alcohol or other drugs must want to quit. The family has nothing to do with it.*

Family's view: "What we do makes no difference. She won't stop until *she* decides to stop."

Professional's view: "This is certainly correct—she must want to abstain and recover. But a part of her decision to quit comes from knowing how her behavior affects others; she must live with the betrayal, guilt, shame, and just plain embarrassment that her chemical use may cause. Family members can help her decide to quit by seeking treatment for themselves, by developing a kind of caring detachment, and by allowing natural consequences to happen. Perhaps the clearest way she can see what she's doing is through the eyes of others."

Family Fallacy #3: *Treatment cures the CD problem.*

Family's view: "Once the CD member gets counseling and education, he will stop having the urge to use, or at least will be able to control his use. With the power of medical science, the doctors and counselors will teach him how to get well.

Professional's view: "There is no medical cure, but like diabetes or hypertension, the disease of chemical dependence can be successfully managed. Although this disease has some important genetic and physical elements, the treatment is not biological—it's educational, emotional, and spiritual. Accepting treatment is the first and most important step, true. But recovery is life-long."

Family Fallacy #4: *When the chemical use stops, the family problems stop.*

Family's view: "Without her being drunk, stoned, belligerent, or sick, and without the loud family arguments and fights because of her use, and with no legal, financial, and job problems caused by the alcohol and other drugs, our family wouldn't have any problems."

Professionals' view: "I agree that many of the urgent and serious problems will disappear. But for a while there could be a kind of 'hangover,' that is, feelings of fear or anger, ill will toward someone, issues about trust and relapse, or concern about how the family will be different now that the CD member is chemical-free. If we can talk about these now, they should be less of a problem for you."

Predictable Family Issues in Early Recovery

In addition to misconceptions about the disease of chemical dependence, several other problems arise frequently in therapy. Therapists should be prepared to encounter them when working with a caseload of CD families. Knowing what to look for can draw attention to these issues before they undermine the early recovery of the family. For all these predictable family issues, the therapist should:
1. Gently educate the family about the issue.
2. Describe it as a normal, natural occurrence in recovering families.
3. Include all the family members in discussing it.
4. If appropriate, encourage the family to make a general plan to handle the problem. Be sure to get the recovering member's agreement to go along with what the family decides.

"Pink Cloud" or "Cloud Nine"

This is the family's flight into health—a rebound from the crises, turmoil, and sickness of the past. Some members may even have an air of super-wellness; they're intensely charging into recovery, as if to make up for lost time.

The recovering CD member is sometimes euphoric: "I feel better than I have in years, and I'm through with drinking forever." Most CD professionals, and certainly AA members, are accustomed to this euphoric high and usually perform a balancing act between celebrating with the individual and cautioning him or her: "Easy does it." "One day at a time." "The higher you go the farther you fall." They remind the newly sober that both extremes—valleys and peaks—can be obstacles on the road to recovery. The most reliable road is level and smooth.

The pink cloud can also engulf other family members. The spouse, older children, parents, or siblings of the CD client can have idealistic expectations about the future and deny the insidious power of the disease. Therapists don't want to destroy the energy and strength that comes from such headstrong optimism, but they should try to slow it down: "I'm always glad to see what we call the 'pink cloud' stage. It shows that you are feeling your potential. I hope you can go slow enough to make it work for you."

Family members who have a more wait-and-see attitude are easier to join with because they are closer to the therapist's view. To them the therapist might say, "I don't blame you for being more cautious. After all, this is a sudden change, and giving it time is a realistic attitude to take."

Lack of Trust

Family members' mistrust of the CD member's sobriety is intrinsic to early recovery. Some members will deny that they have doubts because they know it angers the recovering person, but in their hearts, they are not sure that he or she will stay free of chemicals. Any behavior that resembles the old pattern is suspect, for example, time spent away from home, coming home late, a certain look or tone of voice. If the CD member has unsuccessfully tried to stay sober before, the doubt that "this time will be different" is compounded.

Trust is a critical issue. It can spawn intense arguments and emotion. The CD member doesn't really trust himself or herself, and when someone else mirrors this fear, he or she quickly reacts. Mistrust can even become an excuse for relapse: "If no one trusts me anyway, I might as well keep using."

Trust grows more slowly than some recovering people can tolerate, but the passage of time is essential for rebuilding trust. Sometimes the "time warp" phenomenon occurs during early abstinence. The newly sober person experiences time as passing slowly; a week without his or her drug of choice seems more like a month. To the newly drug-free, a short period of sobriety is a major victory. The family members, however, do not experience this time distortion and are not as impressed by a few weeks of abstinence. Such differing perceptions of time add to the conflict around the trust issue.

Try to make the lack of trust a normal and natural reaction in recovering families by gently predicting that, at one time or another, mistrust will be felt by the family members and that the recovering person will sense this and become angry. Explain that when this happens, everyone will be acting in a perfectly normal and totally expected way.

After talking about mistrust and its transformation into trust with the passage of drug-free time, the therapist can set up a brief exercise. If the family members acknowledge a lack of trust, ask the recovering member, "Are you willing to turn to your family and give them permission *not* to trust you about your alcohol or other drug use for the next six months?" Encourage the the CD member to look the others in the eye and say the words. Bringing the issue of lack of trust into the light of day doesn't make it disappear, but it can reduce its surprise and volatility.

Walking on Eggshells

The predictable problem in early family recovery called "walking on eggshells" is expressed by the family in statements such as, "We can't upset her (the CD member) because it might make her use again." The family is tiptoeing around the CD member, gingerly trying to avoid her anger or displeasure.

As with all of these early recovery issues, the family is never entirely wrong in the way it views the situation. The family may be correct in considering it necessary to keep from "setting the CD member off" and from putting new responsibilities and demands on her too early. The CD member is tentative and shaky with her new sobriety. So is everyone else.

It's just a matter of degree. A certain amount of special consideration is realistic, but too much can turn into enabling, or into allowing the moods of the CD member to dominate the home. In one case, a recovering father had convinced his wife and children to cater to him like servants. He made unyielding rules: no children noises in the house, supper at a precise time each day, and other rigid demands. In therapy, the wife was challenged: "Your husband really needs to be in charge, but will you be able to continue meeting his demands as the months go by?" The husband answered for her, "She's got to. I can only stand so much when I'm sober." His wife stayed silent. Needless to say, the therapist dealt with this important issue in later sessions, beginning by talking with their preteenage children during the family sessions about the house rules. With careful encouragement, one of them was able to say openly that she didn't think the rules were fair. Several minutes of discussion with the three children resulted in more honesty from them which gave the mother more courage to speak out. Slowly and carefully the father was confronted on his demands. This was made possible by the therapist keeping the focus on the topic long enough for it to take on importance and to generate some intensity.

In another case, a recovering chemically dependent man told his wife that if he could not use alcohol or other drugs, he must have sex at least once every day: "Sometimes I need it in the morning, and other times I need it in the afternoons or evenings." In several weeks they had not missed a day. When the therapist commented to the wife that this was a very high rate of sex, she replied, "Yes, but it relaxes him." He had convinced her that recovery depended on her satisfying his sexual whims on demand, regardless of how she felt. In therapy, she never confronted his unrealistic demands, but, again, the therapist talked about it long enough to convey to the couple that her possible resentment was an issue worth watching for in the future.

When the family members are stepping too lightly around the recovering member, the therapist needs to acknowledge their positive intentions of being willing to do whatever it takes to restore the family. At the same time, the therapist should challenge their ability to maintain this delicate treatment and show surprise that the CD member is so powerful. Shine a spotlight on the tight rope the family is walking: "What would happen if you didn't act this way toward him?" or "Are you setting yourself up to be at fault if she uses again?"

IP is in a BUD

BUD is an acronym for "building up to drink." BUD describes a recovering person's restless, irritable, or sullen moods, accompanied by a re-emergence of denial, which often precede a relapse. It is what AA calls "stinking thinking": "I've demonstrated my control over alcohol. Drinking this one time won't hurt since I'll never let myself return to the way I was."

The recovering person often doesn't realize that he or she is in a BUD. Some will deny any shift in mood or thinking, and yet their behavior clearly shows changes in both. A treatment professional, group member, or family member can often see what the recovering person cannot. The reactions and feedback from others is the only mirror available to the recovering person.

After working with recovering people for a while, therapists can sense a BUD. The CD person becomes more agitated, bored, restless, quick-tempered, less tolerant. Or the person becomes unusually quiet, preoccupied, and withdrawn. The telltale sign is a relatively sudden mood or behavior change in any direction.

Therapists should tell families about a BUD, what it is, how it's identified, and what to do with it. If a family member spots the BUD before the CD member does, what will he or she do? Will the CD member give the family permission to gently remind him or her of a change in his or her mood or thinking? Is it okay for the family members to talk with each other when they see it happening and suggest ways to handle the problem? The CD member's permission should be obtained for whatever plan the family makes.

Enabling

Enabling is so pervasive in CD families that it deserves a second look. We've already examined it in Chapter 2, under the topic of changing family patterns that could work against recovery. Enabling is presented here to focus attention on its causes and on a broader, systemic approach to its interruption.

Very few family members, friends, and co-workers who enable intend to contribute to the devastation CD wreaks on a person, even though this may be the sad result. Then why does enabling happen?

Ignorance is one cause. The disease concept of chemical dependence has still not filtered down to the person on the street. In one of my early cases, the single father of a nineteen-year-old client in an inpatient treatment unit came to take his son home for a weekend visit. Since the father lived some distance away, he had not been in the family education component of the treatment program. During our session, the father casually mentioned that he had brought a six-pack of beer for the two of them to drink on their return trip, to lubricate the father's "honest talk with my son about his future." After recovering my power of speech, I did some gentle on-the-spot education about chemical dependence, laws about driving while under the influence, and the father's important contribution to his son's recovery. The father kept his beer cooler locked in the trunk during their trip home, but his sincere and abysmal ignorance left an unforgettable impression.

Enabling also occurs by default, especially between friends and co-workers. No attempt is made to talk about the alcohol or other drug problem. No one wants to confront a person with something that will make him or her angry and defensive, and possibly damage one's relationship with the person. "It's not my business," the reasoning goes. "He can do what he wants." "Who am I to try to control her life? Why, I enjoy alcohol too, and maybe even get high sometimes." When these reasons turn into rationalizations, they delay for months or years any confrontation (caring or otherwise) between personal friends or family and the CD member.

Some enabling is caused by the resistance of a friend, spouse, or other family member to changes made by the CD member. In one case, a CD wife returned home after her inpatient treatment to a husband who handed her a drink of bourbon. He said, "Honey, I know the past few weeks have been hard on you. This will help you relax." Fortunately, the wife refused the liquor, foiling her husband's attempt to restore his drinking partner.

Alcohol and other drug use can become part of the game-playing power struggles of some spouses, leading to another form of enabling. In one family session, the wife described how she kept the alcohol hidden from her husband as a way to control his intake. Her hiding spots, she explained, were clever and undetectable. "I always hide it under the clothes in the old trunk in the attic just to the left at the top of the ladder," she exclaimed to everyone present—including her husband. So much for her "secret" hiding place. Was this couple playing a lethal game with alcohol? After understanding their relationship better, it became obvious that the wife subtly cooperated in her husband's alcoholism. It gave her power over him, and in the eyes of her family and friends, his drinking made her a suffering martyr and him a drunk.

From such accounts, therapists learn that blatant enabling can occur, and that it is vital to include the primary family members in treatment.

A Systems View of Enabling

Enabling is typically defined as behaviors by family members, friends, or others that shield the chemically dependent person from experiencing the harmful consequences of his or her alcohol or other drug use, thereby encouraging the use to continue.

In many cases, enabling is part of a chemical dependent's network. A systems view of enabling looks at, and *beyond*, the prime enabler, or co-dependent, who is usually a spouse or parent. Consider the network in Figure 9.1.

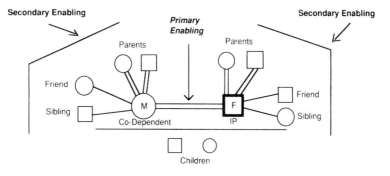

Figure 9.1. Enabling Network

The primary enabler, or co-dependent, is the wife. Others in the CD member's (the IP's) life are serving as secondary enablers: the father's parents, friend, and sibling. On the co-dependent wife's side are the same influential relationships: parents, friend, and sibling. In the above network, all the relationships could be acting as secondary enablers, either directly by enabling the CD member, or indirectly by enabling his co-dependent wife.

If possible, try to get all the people who have a significant relationship with the wife to attend a family session. If they all can't attend, meet with whoever will. The Brief Network Intervention (see Chapter 5) is one way to do this. The purpose of the meeting is to ask the extended family to offer help to the recovering family. The therapist needs to urge the co-dependent's parents, sibling, and friend to provide consistent support to her so she can learn to react to her husband in non-enabling ways. The therapeutic strategy is to use the influences of the co-dependent wife's important relationships to stop her from enabling her husband.

Also, the secondary enablers of the CD member could be part of the same session or part of a different session, depending on the therapist's knowledge of the various alliances between these extended family members. The purpose of that meeting would be the same: to provide help to the family when the going gets tough. For example, during the meeting the therapist might say to the CD client's enabling parents: "Your daughter-in-law has a plan on how to react to your son if he continues to use alcohol or other drugs. Will you be able to help her follow through with her plan if she temporarily weakens?" The strategy is simple: Change the secondary enablers by getting them to help the prime enabler or co-dependent stop enabling.

The CD Member Does Not Abstain

This is not the same as a relapse. A relapse, or "slip," is an incident of alcohol or other drug use during a period when the CD member has decided to and is trying to abstain. In contrast, in early therapy, when the CD member has not decided to and does not abstain, he or she has not yet *attempted* to quit. The CD member continues to drink or take other drugs during treatment, with only minor adjustments in his or her pattern of use. If the CD member is in a treatment program, the staff will eventually find this out, but the family already knows. The family closely monitors the CD member's alcohol or other drug use. Family monitoring is one of the side benefits of including families in treatment.

What does the family therapist do when he or she learns that the CD member is not abstaining? If the CD member is in an outpatient program and is not successfully abstaining, the therapist can talk to the CD member and family about inpatient treatment, giving them information on the treatment centers in the area.

Most CD members strongly resist the idea of inpatient treatment. We need to remember, however, that separate treatment and abstinence for the CD member is the first priority in family therapy for chemical dependence. It is pointless to continue treating the family "symptoms" of CD problems while the alcohol or other drug use remains active. But how long does a therapist wait before he or she starts applying pressure for inpatient treatment? That depends on the case, but if there is no serious attempt at abstinence after three or four family sessions, the time is ripe. If legal leverage is available, it should be used.

If legal pressure is not available, we have a different situation. The CD member who continues using is not interested in recovery—he or she is in outpatient treatment to get someone off his or her back or to get out of some kind of trouble at work or at school. When this happens, the direction to take depends on whether the CD member is an adult spouse or a child living at home.

If the Non-abstaining IP Is a Spouse

In this situation, a major goal for the therapist is to avoid siding with the non-using spouse against the CD member. If the CD member is a husband, for example, and he feels that everyone, including the therapist, is joined in a chorus of confrontation about his chemical use, he is likely to drop out of family sessions. Although the therapist may confront gently with skill and professionalism, it's still an attempt to pressure the husband to change, and generally he experiences this as another form of nagging. Siding with the non-using spouse is perhaps one of the most common errors in CD family therapy: the therapist unintentionally becomes another nagging spouse or parent.

Thankfully, the systems orientation helps the therapist avoid this trap by keeping the alcohol or other drug use in a relationship context: The wife's *reaction* to her husband's alcohol or other drug use can be as much a problem as is the use itself; use and reaction to use are intermixed and interdependent, each one tending to maintain the other.

In such situations therapists need to keep in mind that they are treating two illnesses at once. The co-dependence deserves as much attention as the chemical dependence. If therapy progresses into the third or fourth session and the CD client continues to use, say something like the following to the spouse: "It's becoming clear that your husband has made his choice to use alcohol. But you have choices, too." This maneuver—switching the identified patient— shifts the spotlight from his drinking to *her reaction* to his drinking, thus introducing the wife's part in the equation. Hereafter, the therapy work will include the behaviors of both partners.

This move must be done with gentle respect for the co-dependent's position and emotional dilemma. In the example above, the wife has good reasons for maintaining her co-dependent relationship, no matter how illogical or self-defeating her reasons may appear to the therapist. If she does not as yet have a separate recovery program, this is the first priority. "The only way he will change is if you change yourself" is the therapeutic byline. Getting the co-dependent to seek recovery for herself is the therapeutic goal. This maneuver is a strong intervention and should not be done too early, since prematurely shifting the focus to another family member can cause the therapy to fail. *

---

* For more information on co-dependence, read *Diagnosing and Treating Co-Dependence: A Guide for Professionals Who Work with Chemical Dependents, Their Spouses and Children* by Timmen Cermak, M.D., Johnson Institute, 1986.

If the Non-abstaining IP Is a Child

If the non-abstaining CD member is a child living at home (regardless of age), and no legal leverage is available, the therapist should work with the parenting relationship. The goal is to get the parents to decide together, as a *parental unit*, how much they will tolerate—how far they will allow their child's chemical dependence to progress—before they take firm action to protect their family, themselves, and their CD son or daughter. This becomes the major theme in the family sessions. (For single-parent families, see Chapter 3 for the therapeutic direction in such cases.)

How long parents take to do this will vary widely. I have worked with parents who have set and enforced firm limits within three sessions; others take five to ten sessions. One family went eighteen sessions and never did it. In my experience, the average is about four to eight sessions. If parents do decide to take firm action and present an ultimatum to their child, they will usually do it within two months.

The best intervention in such cases is the least intrusive one. Always start with the least severe measures and only gradually increase severity. Actions that parents can take when their child continues to use alcohol or other drugs while living at home—beginning with the least severe—are:

1. Talking, lecturing, and giving good advice.
2. Setting clear and measurable consequences (removing privileges, restriction, etc.) and *enforcing* them.
3. Refusing to give the child money except for the basic needs.
4. Not rescuing if the child gets in school trouble.
5. Not rescuing if the child gets in legal trouble.
6. Locking the child out of the house after curfew.
7. Calling the police for illegal activities such as driving while impaired, assault, or property damage.
8. If the child is eighteen or older, giving him or her the ultimatum: "We love you and we want to help. But if you continue to use alcohol or other drugs in any amount while living with us, you

must either go to inpatient treatment or leave home."

9. If the child is a minor, taking out a petition through a judge, declaring him or her an "undisciplined child" (or similar terminology). Depending on the local jurisdiction, the child may then be taken from the home and placed in a training school or other institution.

10. Legal commitment to inpatient treatment because of danger to self or others.

Some of these actions may seem harsh. Except in rare cases, however, most parents are not forced to take the most extreme measures. Nevertheless, it's important for the therapist to discuss all the options with the parents, including the most drastic ones, so that they understand that they have the social, ethical, moral, and legal sanctions to set limits. In some cases, parents also need to know that if they don't take steps to intervene, their child is in danger of injuring himself or herself or someone else, of being imprisoned, or, possibly, of dying.

When working this way, be sure that *both* parents agree with the limit-setting, the consequences, and the ultimatum. Parents-as-a-unit can only go as fast as the slower member. Watch carefully for the parent who passively follows the strict member but who silently disagrees with the plan. The passive member's unspoken message to his or her spouse is, "It's your plan and I don't agree with it. And if it doesn't work or something horrible happens, it's your fault."

No one can guarantee the parents good results by taking this approach. However, since the behaviors associated with teenage alcohol or other drug use are the largest single cause of injury and death in this age group, the results of taking no firm action are even more scary. The outcome of the parents' actions is something no one can predict. Explain to the parents that taking stern limit-setting measures is like a dark room, the contents of which are unknown. Warn the parents, "Either go into the dark room holding hands, or don't go in." If one parent carries out a plan—with the silent disagreement of the other—and the son or daughter comes to harm, accidentally or otherwise, the resulting guilt, blame, and anger will most likely damage the spousal relationship and the family. *

Other Issues to Watch For

Sexual Problems

Professionals in the CD field are sometimes hesitant to deal with the subject of sex in therapy sessions. Most CD therapists have had little or no training in sexual dysfunction and sex therapy and need education, training, and desensitization to sexual topics before becoming comfortable enough to discuss this subject with clients.

However, in CD family therapy, certain questions about sex should be asked, especially when the chemically dependent family member is a spouse. During early recovery, a mutually satisfactory sexual relationship between the spouses would be the exception, not the rule. The anger, detachment, physiological impairment, and possible affairs on one or both sides of the relationship all contribute to destroying a couples' sex life, often long before the couple comes to treatment.

Many couples will not mention a sexual problem unless the therapist brings it up first. To do so, a possible opening remark is, "One important part of a marriage is how you function together sexually. Even though you did not present this as a problem, it's too important not to mention. Do either of you have any concerns you want to talk about?" Of course, when discussing any aspect of the spouses' intimate relationship, ask their permission to remove their children from the room, or wait to discuss the topic during an appointment with only the parents. Also, the topic should not be initiated by the therapist

---

* For more information on intervention with chemically dependent adolescents, read *Choices and Consequences: What to Do When A Teenager Uses Alcohol/Drugs*, by Dick Schaefer, Johnson Institute, 1987.

until good rapport and trust has been established with the couple.

If one or both partners admit to sexual dissatisfaction, the therapist needs to inquire further to determine whether the problem can be resolved on a communication level in couples therapy, or if specific sex therapy is needed. Therapists can ask the following questions when making this assessment.

1. How often do you have sexual contact together? Is this frequency satisfactory to you both?
2. Who usually initiates sexual activity?
3. Have either of you noticed any change in your desire to have sex now that the chemical use has stopped?
4. Do you talk together about your sexual relationship?

If either partner shows sustained reluctance to continue on this topic, suggest separate interviews to obtain more information. This could be done with the help of an opposite-sex colleague so that a male therapist interviews the husband, a female interviews the wife. Assure the couple at the beginning of the individual interviews that nothing will be revealed to the other partner without explicit permission.

During the separate interviews, determine whether referral to a qualified sex therapist is needed and desired. If sobriety has been maintained for a few weeks and a primary sexual problem is present (impotence, frigidity, premature ejaculation, etc.), refer the couple to a qualified sex therapist. They may not follow up on this immediately, but the referral is a future option if their sexual problems continue.

AA/NA Triangulation

Triangulation is the systemic term for a common dynamic between two people in conflict. An example is when children become the third part of a triangle with their parents and are used as buffers or substitute battlegrounds through which parents displace deep-seated problems in their marriage. The mother and father have conflicts and arguments about how the other treats the children instead of dealing with how they treat each other. Any person, thing, or activity can be brought into the conflict and argued about, thus serving as a buffer zone for the couple to avoid the relationship problems and the disagreements between them. Work is a common triangulated activity, and so are pets, sports, television, hobbies, or anything else people do.

Alcohol or other drug use is common as a triangulated activity, but even when this stops, AA or NA or the treatment center itself may be triangulated to take its place. Instead of dealing directly with each other about their relationship difficulties, the spouses may argue about the recovering member staying away from home with his or her AA meetings in the same way he or she used to distance himself or herself with the alcohol or other drugs.

One wife summed up the situation between herself and her husband by saying, "He's sober, but now he's addicted to AA." This couple spent much of the family sessions arguing about the husband's obsession with AA and how it separated him from the family. The wife had a legitimate complaint ("You're never home"), and the husband had a perfect defense ("Meetings keep me sober"). This doesn't happen as often when the CD member is a child, since most parents are usually eager for their child to be intensely involved in a recovery program.

When AA, NA, or the treatment program becomes the couple's battleground, the therapist can take a gentle but definite stand. First, acknowledge the non-using spouse's disappointment and frustration. Then remind the couple that sobriety is the first and most important goal, and that they are fortunate to have found a way to achieve this. Explain that people in early recovery often pour themselves into their treatment with the same passion they once had for their drug of choice. But passionate recovery is far better than passionate use, and it just may have to be that way for a while. Also, talk with the non-using spouse about his or her own recovery, emphasizing the importance of and the support to be found at Al-Anon or Naranon.

Subtle Blackmailing

Occasionally, the recovering CD member attempts to force compli-ance from family members by threatening to use alcohol or other drugs again if things don't go his or her way. The threats can be indirect and don't need to be explicit to be effective: "If you keep doing this, I don't know how I can handle it" or "This is driving me crazy" or other threatening innuendos are often enough to achieve control.

This happens frequently with an adolescent CD member whose parents are intimidated by their teenager's stated or implied threat to go back to using or to run away from home if the parents don't give in on a particular issue. When parents succumb to any of this hostage-taking, they lose control of the situation. They also lose their chance to be a positive influence on their child's recovery.

Blackmailing is a nasty term but its results are even nastier. If an instance of blackmailing comes up in a session, take a definite stand: "Let me be clear about my opinion on this. Sometimes a recovering person will blackmail others by making them believe that they can cause him or her to use alcohol or other drugs. Only the CD member can make herself or himself use. No one else can do that. If you let threats control you, you will lose your chance to be a strong defense against a stubborn disease." This can be said with or without the "blackmailer" present, depending on the therapist's judgment. Keep the responsibility for the CD member's recovery directly on the CD member and away from other family members. If anyone else takes on that burden for the CD member, the family is back to enabling, co-dependence, and heartbreak.

"Sponsorship" by a Family Member

Sometimes a spouse or parent inadvertently takes on the role of an AA or NA sponsor or a professional counselor with the recovering mem-ber. He or she monitors treatment progress and attendance at meetings, offers "counseling" and CD education, and is available 24 hours a day

207

for crisis work with the recovering person. If family members are in this role or about to assume this role, therapists need to make it clear that any family member who tries to become the counselor or unofficial sponsor is setting up the relationship for crisis. The family member is not objective enough to mix a family and a professional role, even if the family member *is* a treatment professional. The family member as sponsor puts too much responsibility for the CD member's recovery on the family member, thus taking responsibility away from the CD member—not a healthy recovery practice for either of them. Finally, the family member sponsor and the actual AA or NA sponsor or treatment professional may use different approaches to the problem, putting the CD member in a confusing and conflicting triangle. All this can be avoided if the roles of the professionals and the roles of the family members are clarified and kept separate.

To interrupt spousal sponsorship, tactfully point out to the sponsor member what is happening. Acknowledge his or her caring but overly responsible attitude and explain why it's not a good idea. Ask for the recovering person's help to convince the spouse to let go of his or her extreme responsibility. This is also an appropriate time to mention Al-Anon or Naranon as a source of support for the sponsor member.

To interrupt parental sponsorship, the parent who is less involved with the CD child can be the therapist's ally. Get this parent to help the sponsor parent take a rest and let the program professionals attend to their child's treatment needs. Emphasize that to help their chemically dependent son or daughter, the parents' responsibilities are to: (1) work out their agreements with each other so their child receives the same clear and consistent recovery and limit-setting message from both parents; (2) attend their own education and recovery groups, either as part of the treatment program or in community self-help groups (Al-Anon, etc.); and (3) attend therapy sessions with their family during and after the primary treatment of their child. If parents do all this, they are doing enough.

Preparing the Family for Possible Relapse

The last session or two of the family treatment is the time to begin talking about the possibilities of relapse. This is not a popular topic with families, but it needs some airing. It can be introduced with a statement such as, "I know you don't want to hear about this, especially at a time when you are doing so well. But, unfortunately, relapse is sometimes part of this disease. My motto is to expect the best and be prepared for the worst. Have you thought about this?"

The family can be gently educated by the therapist's questions about relapse. Since the relapse questions are different, depending on whether the CD member is a parent or a child, here are examples of both.

When the CD member is a married parent, ask:

1. Drinking takes a lot of time. How will you spend the extra time now that you're not using?
2. Will you divide up parenting responsibilities differently?
3. Will your social life change?
4. Will your friends change?
5. Will contact with your extended family change?
6. To the non-chemically dependent spouse:
   a. What do you think might happen if your partner spends more time away from home (at work, church, AA meetings, etc.)?
   b. What will happen if your spouse begins to have mood swings and becomes irritated, angry, withdrawn, or gets depressed?
   c. Do you think your spouse can ever return to normal drinking?
   d. Do you have a plan if a relapse occurs? (Do not ask the spouse to discuss his or her specific plan, since the spouse might not want to reveal to the CD member what he or she will do if a relapse occurs.)

Relapses are handled by the CD member's support group (AA, NA, treatment center program, or other group). The therapist can also get the family to agree to have an immediate family session in case of relapse.

When the CD member is an adolescent, talk with both parents (in a two-parent household), usually without the CD adolescent or other children present. Ask:

1. What are your child's responsibilities and privileges at home?
2. What are your rules of the house (curfew, chores, etc.)?
3. How will you control driving or other privileges until you are certain your child is abstinent?
4. What are some ways your child can earn privileges and begin to reestablish trust?
5. What is your plan if a relapse occurs?
   a. What will you do to convince your child that you're serious?
   b. How will you make agreements together to modify the plan?
   c. How can the plan fail?
6. Can you support each other? When one temporarily weakens, can the other be strong?

Once these questions and issues are discussed and the details of the plan are agreed upon and negotiated (which usually takes more than one session), the parents inform the adolescent of their agreements. These agreements could be written and copies given to parents, child, and therapist. The parents should inform the CD adolescent about the plan during a session, unless the therapist is convinced that it would go more smoothly if done at home. If there is an obvious strict/lenient parent split, ask the lenient parent to do most of the talking. Stern talk from the more lenient parent convinces the CD adolescent that change is in the air.

Procedural Questions

In the systems approach to therapy, the client is the family, not one of its members. This raises a few procedural questions. If a therapist is assigned as the primary counselor for a CD adolescent and the therapist sees him or her individually and in groups, can the same therapist also be the family therapist for that adolescent? Not ideally. The parents will tend to see him or her as their child's therapist, not theirs. This systems model of therapy emphasizes joining well with the parents to help the entire family, including the CD adolescent. If parents are in conflict with their CD child, and they believe that the therapist is more sympathetic with their child's side, how can the therapist join well with the parents? Therapists involved as primary counselors are well advised to let someone else work with the family while they continue individual and/or group therapy with the CD adolescent. Of course, the therapist can be called in to one of the family sessions to better understand the CD adolescent's family situation or participate in Colleague Teamwork (see Chapter 7) in the family sessions.

If a therapist's individual CD client is a married adult, can the therapist act as this person's primary counselor and marriage or family counselor at the same time? If the therapist is seeing the CD client only in groups, the therapist might be able to play both roles. But if the therapist is seeing the CD client individually, this dual role for the therapist not a good idea, primarily because of the assumed (or actual) side-taking by the therapist with the CD client during the marriage or family sessions.

If a therapist is seeing a family with a chemically dependent parent who drops out of the family sessions, should the therapist continue with the rest of the family? Yes, at least long enough to start the family in its own recovery program. But the therapist should also try to reengage the CD parent. Talk with him or her on the phone, continue to hear his or her side of the story, and invite him or her to participate. In cases like this, therapists must be careful not to set up a dangerous "us against you" situation in the CD parent's mind.

If therapists do all they can do, and the CD member continues using but also continues to come for family sessions, what then? Stay with it. As long as the CD member is attending with the family, there is hope. If therapists keep the family in therapy, something worthwhile almost always happens.

EPILOGUE
The Craft and Art of Family Therapy

In a casual conversation, a friend once said to me, "Sometimes I feel so good I just want to burst out in song. But I can't sing!" My friend had the inspiration but not the expression.

This book is about the expression—the techniques and methods for helping CD families begin to get well. Much is said about how-to and little about the inspirational, moving, and intuitive moments of therapy. There are plenty of those moments, especially if we are not afraid to allow them, and if we learn to recognize and nurture them. But for this to happen, our intuition—as contradictory as this may sound—needs to be trained and prepared.

Such preparation gives us the craft of our profession. A mastery of the fundamentals and a storehouse of experiences makes possible the artistic side of therapy, the spontaneity and the creativity. The separate skills, acquired through intelligent practice, must exist before they can combine into something intuitive and creative. Anyone who has labored to learn the skills of a complex art form—playing music, painting, dancing, writing, and others—will know what I mean.

Many of my colleagues in training want to know the art before learning the craft. I don't blame them; I was impatient, too. They want to know what to do with families without conducting many hours of family therapy, without experimenting with new, systemic ways of thinking, without mastering the fundamentals of careful rapport-building, patience, sensitivity to nuances of expression, timing, pacing, filling an empty silence in the room, and other skills that come with study and practice. They naively believe they can skip some of the steps of learning.

During one training session, a colleague was getting impatient with the details. "All that's interesting, but how do you overcome resistance? My families are very resistant and don't want to change." This dedicated young woman wanted a magic package of answers, neatly wrapped and handed to her. All I could think of to say was, "Ask me again after several months of our work together." Not a very clever response, but I was trying to say that no universal formulas and shortcuts eliminate the need for learning, practice, imitation, and repetition. The cumulative effects of these experiences earn us the mastery of the craft, and ultimately, the art of our profession.

Only then can we put some of our craft-consciousness aside and let more of our spontaneity spill into the session. We are free to be more relaxed and personable, free to enjoy the families, confident that we can somehow manage whatever happens. We have learned our skills well enough to forget them.

When this happens, we enter another stage in our personal and professional growth—learning to be better therapists rather than better technicians.

~~~~~~

There are many reasons to write a book. One of mine was to encourage more professional helpers to conduct therapy with CD families. To do this, I have tried to give some practical guidelines to those who either are already working with CD families now or would like to begin. With the alcohol and other drug epidemic in our country, we desperately need more available, varied, and effective treatments.

The answer to chemical dependence, however, is obviously not found totally in the treatment of the disease. The answer is in changing some of the conditions that give rise to it: poverty and lack of opportunity for the underprivileged, our stress-filled lifestyle, the depersonalization of the individual, and the weakening of the family, to name a few. These are mostly social problems, and they await cultural and political solutions, often a fatally slow process. To save lives now, we need better treatment for the many people who can benefit from it.

In treating chemical dependence, we need all the approaches we can find. Individual therapy has not proved to be the treatment of choice for chemical dependence. Group therapy is usually powerful and effective, but sometimes it turns into a covey of affable comrades and loses its therapeutic purpose. AA, NA, co-dependence groups, and other twelve-step approaches, although offering the most help for the most people, are not embraced by everyone who needs them.

Perhaps the same can be said of family therapy. But I am convinced that it's a powerful approach and one that can fit a variety of needs. A major bonus in treating the family is that regardless of what the chemically dependent member chooses to do, one or more other family members may accept your help and find recovery and hope for themselves as individuals and as a family.

For most of us, our families contain the best, the worst, and the most lasting influences in our lives. In the helping professions, I can think of no therapeutic work more important than helping a chemically dependent family make the transition to a recovering family, thus removing one of the cruelest and most devastating influences on people's growth in our society. To help a family make this transition is the most profound and loving gift our profession can offer.

BIBLIOGRAPHY

Books

Anderson, C. M., and S. Stewart *Mastering Resistance: A Practical Guide to Family Therapy.* New York: Guilford Press, 1983.

Barnard, C. P. *Families, Alcoholism, and Therapy.* Springfield, IL: Charles C. Thomas, 1981.

Beavers, W. *Successful Marriage: A Family Systems Approach to Couples Therapy.* New York: W. W. Norton, 1985.

Bepko, C. *The Responsibility Trap: A Blueprint for Treating the Alcoholic Family.* New York: Free Press, 1985.

Berger, M., et. al. *Practicing Family Therapy in Diverse Settings.* San Francisco: Jossey-Bass, 1984.

Bergman, J. *Fishing for Barracuda: Pragmatics of Brief Systemic Therapy.* New York: W. W. Norton, 1985.

Cermak, T. L. *Diagnosing and Treating Co-Dependence.* Minneapolis: Johnson Institute, 1986.

Cermak, T. L. *Evaluating and Treating Adult Children of Alcoholics.* Vols. 1 and 2. Minneapolis: Johnson Institute, 1990.

CruiseJesse, R. C. *Healing the Hurt: Rebuilding Relationships With Your Children.* Minneapolis: Johnson Institute, 1990.

Fishman, H. C. *Treating Troubled Adolescents.* New York: Basic Books, Inc., 1988.

Gurman, A., ed. *Questions and Answers in the Practice of Family Therapy.* New York: Brunner/Mazel, 1981.

Haley, J. *Leaving Home: The Therapy of Disturbed Young People*. New York: McGraw-Hill, 1980.

Haley, J. *Problem Solving Therapy*. 2d ed. San Francisco: Jossey-Bass, 1987.

Hoffman, L. *Foundations of Family Therapy*. New York: Basic Books, 1981.

Johnson, V. E. *I'll Quit Tomorrow*. San Francisco: Harper & Row, 1980.

Johnson, V. E. *Intervention: How to Help Someone Who Doesn't Want Help*. Minneapolis: Johnson Institute, 1986.

Kaufman, E., ed. *Power to Change: Family Case Studies in the Treatment of Alcoholism*. New York: Gardner Press, 1984.

Kaufman, E., and P. Kaufman. *Family Therapy of Drug and Alcohol Abuse*. New York: Gardner Press, 1979.

Lawson, G., et.al. *Alcoholism and the Family*. Rockville, MD: Aspen Systems Corporation, 1984.

Minuchin, S. *Families and Family Therapy*. Cambridge: Harvard University Press, 1974.

Minuchin, S. *Family Kaleidoscope*. Cambridge: Harvard University Press, 1984.

Minuchin, S., and H. Fishman. *Family Therapy Techniques*. Cambridge: Harvard University Press, 1981.

Mirkin, M. P., and S. L. Koman. *Handbook of Adolescents and Family Therapy*. New York: Gardner Press, 1985.

Morawetz, A., and G. Walker. *Brief Therapy With Single-Parent Families*. New York: Brunner/Mazel, 1984.

Sager, C. J. *Treating the Remarried Family*. New York: Brunner/Mazel, 1983.

Satir, V. *Conjoint Family Therapy*. Palo Alto, CA: Science & Behavior Books, 1967.

Schaefer, C., et.al. *Family Therapy Techniques for Problem Behaviors of Children and Teenagers*. San Francisco: Jossey-Bass, 1984.

Sherman, R., and N. Fredman. *Handbook of Structured Techniques in Marriage and Family Therapy*. New York: Brunner/Mazel, 1986.

Stanton, M., and T. Todd. *The Family Therapy of Drug Abuse and Addiction*. New York: Guilford Press, 1982.

Steinglass, P. *The Alcoholic Family*. New York: Basic Books, 1987.

Thomas, L. *Lives of a Cell*. New York: Bantam Books, 1974.

Vaillant, G. *The Natural History of Alcoholism*. Cambridge: Harvard University Press, 1983.

Wegscheider, S. *Another Chance: Hope and Health for the Alcoholic Family*. Palo Alto, CA: Science and Behavior Books, 1981.

Wolman, B., and F. Stricker., eds. *Handbook of Family and Marital Therapy*. New York: Plenum Press, 1983.

Journals

Adolescent Counselor ("Education About Addictions"). 12729 N.E. 20th, Suite 12, Bellevue, WA 98005. Published 6 times per year.

Changes ("For and About Adult Children of Alcoholics"). Health Communications, Inc., 1721 Blount Road, Suite 1, Pompano Beach, FL 33069. Published 6 times per year.

Focus ("On Chemically Dependent Families"). U.S. Journal, Inc., 3201 S.W. 15th St., Deerfield Beach, FL 33442. Published 6 times per year.

Professional Counselor ("Serving the Alcohol and Drug Addictions Field"). 12729 N.E. 20th, Suite 12, Bellevue, WA 98005. Published 6 times per year.

Books

The following books and booklets on chemical dependence and related topics are available from Hazelden, Call 1-800-328-9000.

Timmen L. Cermak, M.D., *Diagnosing and Treating Co-Dependence A Guide for Professionals Who Work with Chemical Dependence, Their Spouses, and Children.*

Vernon E. Johnson, D.D., *Everything You Need to Know about Chemical Dependence.*

Vernon E. Johnson, D.D., *Intervention: How To Help Someone Who Doesn't Want Help: A Step-By-Step Guide for Families and Friends of Chemically Dependent Persons.*

David J. Wilmes, *Parenting for Prevention: How to Raise a Child to Say No to Alcohol/Drugs.*

220

Booklets

Alcoholism: A Treatable Disease. Takes a straightforward look at the disease of alcoholism, the confusion and delusion accompanying it, and the process of intervention, stressing a message of hope: alcoholism *is* treatable.

Chemical Dependence: Yes, You Can Do Something. Gives families of chemical dependents the basic knowledge they need to understand and help their loved ones *now*.

Detachment: The Art of Letting Go While Living with an Alcoholic. Tells how loved ones of the chemically dependent person can learn to take responsibility for themselves, not for the drinker, and rebuild themselves in a way that can restore healthy thinking and lead to serenity, freedom, and peace.

The Dynamics of Addiction. Explains some of the physical and psychological aspects of addiction and describes how an addiction develops and continues.

The Family Enablers. Identifies and addresses the problem of family members who don't deal directly with their lived one's alcoholism and thereby enable him or her to progress to more serious stages of the disease; points the way toward whole-family recovery.

How It Feels to Be Chemically Dependent. Uses hard-hitting language to help break through the denial of chemically dependent persons who can't see what alcohol or other drugs are doing to them; helps give families and friends a clearer understanding of the emotional effects of chemical dependence.

Recovery of Chemically Dependent Families. Examines the high expectations and fears of chemically dependent families and explores how the family can learn to communicate and recover together.

Index

AA (Alcoholics Anonymous), viii
  role of, in long-term support, 40-41
  triangulation technique with, 205-206
Adolescent patient
  dealing with relapse in, 210-212
  during second family therapy session, 187
  in enmeshed child IP pattern, 67-69
  Guardrail exercise with, 135-136
  involvement of both parents in treatment for, 158-161
  non-abstention in, 202-204
  parental overinvolvement with, 159
  safe rebellion technique and, 129-130
Adult Children of Alcoholics (ACOA), 41
Age of IP, as factor, in CD family therapy, 61
Al-Anon, 52
  defined, viii
  in long-term support, 40-41
  in Peripheral Parent IP pattern, 64
Alateen
  defined, viii
  role of, in long-term support, 40-41
Alter ego technique, 3, 111-113
  during third session of family therapy, 188
  variations in, 113
"Analysis paralysis," 123
Anger
  during early recovery, 39
  Good Child/Bad Child pattern and, 71-72
  joining and, 94-97
  role of, in Single Parent IP pattern, 87

Anxiety
  chemical dependence and, 25-26
  of IP, over family sessions, 26-27
  See also Shame.
Assessment techniques, during second family therapy session, 187
Attendance policies, for family therapy, 163
Audiotapes, for family members missing from therapy sessions, 172
Behavior
  compulsive, 28, 137-138
  emphasis on, in systems therapy, 18-19, 150
  enabling and, 34-35
  individualist approach to therapy and, 10
  safe rebellion technique and, 129-130
Biological parent
  in adolescent patient therapy, 161-162
  in Blended Family-Child IP pattern, 77-78
  in Blended Family - Stepparent IP, 79-81
  in Single Parent - Child IP, 83-84
Blackmailing, during therapy sessions, 207
  Good Child/Bad Child pattern and, 72
Blame
  prevalence of, in Blended Family - Stepparent IP, 79-81
  role of, in systems orientation, 18-19

223

Scapegoating
  Good Child/Bad Child pattern and,
    70-73
  "whole-family message" of systems
    therapy, 31-32
Sculpting technique, 132-133
  during second family therapy
    session, 187
Seating arrangements
  changes in, during third session of
    family therapy, 188
  Changing the Distance exercise and,
    134
  enactment technique and, 104
  for initial interview, 182
  mapping technique and, 48
  Place Yourself exercise and, 135
Second session of family therapy,
    185-188
See-saw families, Single Parent IP
    pattern and, 85
Segmenting technique, 105-108
  during second family therapy
    session, 187
Self-help recovery groups, 91
Sexual abuse
  revealed by segmenting technique,
    107
  role of, in Blended Family -
    Stepparent IP, 80
Sexual problems, as issue during
    therapy sessions, 204-205
Shame
  impact of, on family therapy
    sessions, 157
  joining technique and, 95-97
Sibling conflicts
  in chemically dependent families,
    17-18
  in enmeshed child IP pattern, 69

Good Child/Bad Child pattern and,
    70-73
importance of, in adolescent therapy,
    158
in Single Parent - Child IP, 83-84
Sidetaking by therapist
  non-abstaining CD patient and, 200-
    201
  as stumbling block to therapy, 140-
    141
Simplicity, role of, in family therapy,
    153
Single family sessions, scheduling of,
    in systems therapy, 23
Single Parent - Child IP pattern, 81-
    84
Single Parent IP pattern, 85-87
Single-parent families
  CD therapy in, 61
  peripheral CD family members and,
    37-38
"Small-talk," role of, during initial
    interview, 175-176
Social stage, initial interview, 175-
    176, 184
Solo role of therapist, as stumbling
    block to
    systems therapy, 144-154
Spousal relations
  dating and, 99
  Good Child/Bad Child pattern and,
    72
  non-abstaining CD patient and, 200-
    201
  reciprocity in, 140
  role of, in patterns, 92
  treatment sponsors in, 207-208
Stability
  denial and resistance as tools for, 60
  role of, in families, 8-9
Stair-stepping phenomenon, 69

Three-session therapy commitment,
    by family members, 180
Tough Love, role of, in long-term
    support, 40-41
Treatment sponsorship by family
    member, 207-208
  in enmeshed child IP pattern, 68-69
  in Parent in the Middle pattern, 66-
    67
  in Single Parent - Child IP, 83-84
Triangulated Child IP pattern, 73-75
Triangulation technique for systems
    therapy, 205-206
Trust
  lack of, during early recovery, 192-
    193
  vs. technique, 109
Twelve-step process
  enabling and, 35
  role of, in systems therapy, 40-41

Two-parent households, recruiting
    techniques, for
    family therapy sessions, 158-159
Unpredictability, in CD families, 60
Videotaping, during systems therapy,
    147
Visitation rights, role of, in Divorced
    - Child IP pattern, 88
"Walking on eggshells" phase of
    early recovery, 193-194
*What to Do When A Teenager Uses
    Alcohol/Drugs*, 204
"Whole-family-message" in systems
    therapy, 29-32, 163-164
Withdrawal, emotional, during early
    recovery, 39

About Hazelden Publishing

As part of the Hazelden Betty Ford Foundation, Hazelden Publishing offers both cutting-edge educational resources and inspirational books. Our print and digital works help guide individuals in treatment and recovery, and their loved ones. Professionals who work to prevent and treat addiction also turn to Hazelden Publishing for evidence-based curricula, digital content solutions, and videos for use in schools, treatment programs, correctional programs, and electronic health records systems. We also offer training for implementation of our curricula.

Through published and digital works, Hazelden Publishing extends the reach of healing and hope to individuals, families, and communities affected by addiction and related issues.

For more information about Hazelden publications,
please call **800-328-9000**
or visit us online at **hazelden.org/bookstore**.